101 THINGS YOU
and John McCain
DIDN'T KNOW ABOUT
SARAH PALIN

Gregory Bergman

with Paula Munier

Avon, Massachusetts

Copyright © 2008 by F+W Media, Inc.
All rights reserved.
This book, or parts thereof, may not be reproduced in any form without
permission from the publisher; exceptions are made for brief excerpts
used in published reviews.

Published by
Adams Media, an F+W Media Company
57 Littlefield Street, Avon, MA 02322. U.S.A.
www.adamsmedia.com

ISBN 10: 1-60550-995-7
ISBN 13: 978-1-60550-995-2

Printed in the United States of America.

J I H G F E D C B A

Library of Congress Cataloging-in-Publication Data
is available from the publisher.

Interior illustration credits:
American flag © iStockphoto / RichVintage
Notebook © iStockphoto / rusm
Microphone © iStockphoto / DawnPoland
Index card © iStockphoto / belterz
Alaska outline © Map Resources

This book is available at quantity discounts for bulk purchases.
For information, please call 1-800-289-0963.

This book is dedicated to both
my mother and Sarah Palin,
without whom this book would
not have been possible.

CONTENTS

Part 1

THE MANY FACES OF
SARAH PALIN

The Republicans have anointed Sarah Palin "Wal-Mart Mom of the Election." And it's playing well in Peoria. Not to mention Wasilla.

In 1996, the Soccer Moms were the key swing votes. In 2004, it was the Security Moms. And now, thanks to the in-your-face discount charm of Sarah Palin, the Wal-Mart Moms are expected to have the last word on November 4.

Who are the Wal-Mart Moms? According to *Time* magazine, they're the forty- to fifty-something moms and grandmoms of the so-called Sandwich Generation—caught between their aging parents and their growing kids and charged with caregiving them all. They're stressed, they're broke, and most of all, they're *tired.* Which helps us understand the love affair: Only battle fatigue could explain why they've fallen for Sarah Palin.

Palin aside, Wal-Mart Moms are a relatively new phenomenon in Alaska, where Wal-Mart opened its first supercenter in Juneau on September 12, 2007.

"The store is designed to save shoppers both time and money," Store Manager Kai Kauai said at the time. "It's exciting to bring something new to our residents, but also be able to offer tourists something they are familiar with."

Yes, something tourists will be familiar with—like Western Civilization. Or at least what passes for it in the red states.

THINK ABOUT THIS

According to Walmart.com, "Our environmental goals are simple and straightforward: To be supplied 100 percent by renewable energy; to create zero waste; and to sell products that sustain our resources and the environment."

We know, we didn't believe it either. Which is harder to swallow: Wal-Mart's self-proclaimed dedication to saving the earth or Sarah Palin's commitment to destroying it?

SARAH STAT

According to the Wal-Mart website, properties in Alaska include 3 supercenters, 5 discount stores, and 3 Sam's Clubs. The company employs 3,163 Alaskans at an average pay of $12.57 an hour. Not bad for Wasilla, where the average job pays only $16.93 an hour—and the unemployment rate is a whopping 11.2 percent, nearly double the national rate. Which is why Sarah Palin really, really, really loves Wal-Mart.

WHY SARAH PALIN LOVES WAL-MART

★ They have a fully loaded gun department
★ You can buy live bait there
★ Ammo is always priced at "buy five, shoot the sixth bastard for free"
★ The sushi bar is catch-it-yourself
★ You'll find the latest in camouflagewear there
★ Beaver's on sale for only $4.99 a pound—but remember, it's even cheaper if you shoot it yourself (just ask Sarah) *

*See fully loaded gun department

Wal-Mart Mom's
Special Slow Cooker
Barbecued Beaver

Serves
8

This is a double-cooked slow-cooker recipe. Do the first cooking overnight, which cooks the meat until tender. The next day, remove fat and bones (if any). The lean meat is put back to simmer in the barbecue sauce. Yummy!

1 (4- to 5-pound) beaver roast(s)

4–5 cloves garlic, minced

Kosher salt and freshly ground black pepper to taste

3 onions, sliced and divided

6 whole cloves

2 cups hot water

1 (16-ounce) bottle of spicy barbecue sauce

8 sandwich buns, kaiser rolls, or hoagie rolls

1. Rub roast with garlic and season with salt and pepper to taste. Place one-third of the onion slices in the bottom of a slow cooker. Cover with roast. Place one-third of the onions on top of the roast. Add cloves and water. Cover and cook on low for 10–12 hours or until meat is tender.
2. Place meat on a baking sheet and remove fat and any bones. Empty the slow cooker.
3. Place one-third of the onions on the bottom of the slow cooker. Add cleaned meat and barbecue sauce. Cook on low for 4 to 8 hours or cook on high for 1 to 3 hours.
4. Toast buns and serve with barbecued meat.

Sarah's Cooking Tips

This barbequed beaver pays for itself—and more!—if you sell the beaver skin, which can bring a handsome sum due to its prized fur. Note: Under Alaskan law, when you hunt or trap beaver, "either the meat or the hide of the beaver must be salvaged." (2008–2009 Alaska Hunting Regulations)

Radio talk show host Stephanie Miller dubbed Sarah Palin "Caribou Barbie"—and the name has stuck.

Mattel may not be thrilled, and Santa Claus even less so, but the spectre of our svelte Sarah Palin armed to slaughter Old St. Nick's reindeer is titillating disturbed Americans from Nome to New York City. Now this is where all you Caribou Barbie fans proclaim loudly, "But I didn't know caribou was the NRA code name for reindeer!" Sure, like everyone doesn't know that Webster defines the word like this:

car*i*bou
a large, gregarious (read: happy, until you shoot it) deer of Holarctic taiga and tundra that typically boasts palmate antlers in both sexes, especially in the New World—also called reindeer.

Also called reindeer. You read it here first. Caribou Barbie is just an NRA euphemism for Rudolph-the-Red-Nosed Serial Killer. That said, here's a nice reindeer recipe you can whip up for Christmas Eve, should you be sitting down to Praise the Lord with Republicans.

SARAH STAT

Caribou hunting is a family tradition. In fact, Sarah Palin's parents, Sally and Charles Heath, were out hunting for Santa's reindeer when her nomination was announced. "The river was swollen, so we almost didn't get back," Sally explained to *CBS News*. I hate that when that happens to my folks. Not that it ever does, since like most retired Americans, they live in Las Vegas.

Secret Santa Sarah's
Beer-Braised Reindeer Roast

Serves
4-6

Think outside of the box when it comes to braising liquids. Instead of beer or red wine, try cranberry juice, apple cider, or even cola.

1 (5- to 6-pound) caribou roast

1 tablespoon German-style grainy mustard

1 teaspoon garlic salt

1 teaspoon freshly ground black pepper

1 beer (wheat or pale ale)

1. Preheat oven to 350°F.
2. Rub roast with mustard and sprinkle with garlic salt and pepper.
3. Place in a roasting pan and bake, uncovered, for ½ hour. Add the beer and cover the pan. Lower the heat to 275°F and baste every 20 minutes. Cook for about 3 or 4 hours or until meat is tender and done to your liking.

Sarah's Cooking Tip

If you're worried that the sight of you devouring reindeer just as Santa and Rudolph take to the sky for their yearly visit might upset your little ones, wait till New Year's to make this recipe.

YOU MIGHT BE A CARIBOU BARBIE IF:

★ You have your taxidermist on speed dial.

★ There are more antlers than family pictures on your walls.

★ You've ever shot anyone just for looking at you funny.

★ You own a homemade fur coat.

★ You have "ammo" on your Christmas list.

★ You've ever scarfed down more than three moose burgers in a sitting.

#3 Sarah Palin supports funding for abstinence-only programs in schools. Just call her Grandma.

Unless you've been living in a cave (or Alaska), you know that Sarah Palin's seventeen-year-old daughter Bristol is having eighteen-year-old Levi Johnston's baby—which proves that "just say no" doesn't work when you're talking to an oversexed teenager. And they're *all* oversexed. Just ask Freud.

Sex aside, Palin is proud of her daughter's devotion to Christianity and Christian values. Neighbors have reportedly been awakened at night by her passionate prayers: "Oh my God!," "Jesus, that's good," and "Praise the Lord!"

FOR A GOOD TIME, CALL 1-800-BRISTOL

According to studies at Yale and Columbia Universities, kids in virginity pledge programs (translation: just say no until you're married) are more likely than their peers to have unprotected sex. These abstaining teens are also *six* times more likely to have oral sex and *four* times more likely to have anal sex.

SARAH SAYS:

"We're proud of Bristol's decision to have her baby and even prouder to become grandparents."

—SARAH AND TODD PALIN

#4 In 2007 Sarah Palin offered $150 to every hunter who hacked off the left foreleg of a wolf shot from a plane. Talk about wolves being thrown, uh, to the wolves.

Sarah's freezer is full of caribou and moose meat that she shot herself. But she's campaigned for the aerial shooting of wolves arrogant enough to do the same thing.

The Federal Airborne Hunting Act of 1972 made aerial wolf hunting illegal for hunters—spoilsports! But don't get your camouflage panties in a bunch, there's a loophole. State governments can give out permits to state employees or licensed individuals for the sake of protecting "land, water, wildlife, livestock, domesticated animals, human life, or crops." Thus ensuring a lifetime of moose burgers for all. Except, of course, the wolf.

WHERE THERE'S A WOLF . . .
But leave it to our piece-packing girl to make the most of the lupe loophole. When she took office as governor, gunning down wolves from planes turned into a for-profit game! In 2007, in an effort to boost the bloodsport, she offered $150 to every hunter who hacked off the left foreleg of a wolf shot from a plane. A state judge went on to overrule the payments, but not the aerial shooting. So get on up there to Alaska, and shoot yourself a wolf while you still can!

To wit: Sarah Palin is a card-carrying Wolf Hater. And she's proud of it. Statie aside, show her a severed wolfie paw and she'll fork over a hundred and fifty bucks—no questions asked (just don't tell the state judge who overturned the bounty). *Note:* What you do with the rest of the wolf is your business—apparently Palin believes they're not very good eatin'. For a real meal, you need to bag yourself a moose.

Sarah Barracuda
Moose Burgers with Condiment Bar

Serves 8

2 pounds ground moose

Coarse kosher salt and freshly cracked black pepper to taste

8 or 10 buns, buttered and toasted

1 head romaine lettuce, washed and torn

1 red onion, thinly sliced

2 beefsteak tomatoes, thinly sliced

2 avocados, peeled and sliced

1 cup Kalamata olives, chopped

Assorted cheeses, crumbled, sliced, or shaved (Boursin, Cheddar, blue, pecorino, goat, Monterey jack, etc.)

1 pound bacon, fried crisp

Assorted spreads: mustard, mayonnaise, ketchup, barbecue sauce, etc.

(continued)

1. Form meat into 8 to 10¾-inch-thick patties. Place on a baking sheet. Sprinkle with coarse salt and cracked pepper to taste. Turn patties over and repeat the seasoning. Refrigerate for an hour so the meat will hold together on the grill.
2. Place breads and buns in a basket.
3. Arrange lettuce, onion, tomatoes, avocados, olives, sliced cheeses, and bacon on a platter. Place crumbled and shaved cheeses in bowls. Set spreads out in the bottles for a casual get-together or transfer to serving bowls for a fancier party.
4. Prepare a hot fire in the grill. Sear burgers over high heat for about 2 or 3 minutes per side for medium-rare. Cook longer for more well-done. Place on a platter and serve with all the fixings.

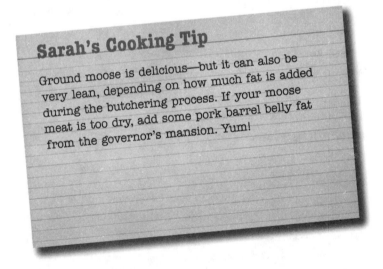

Sarah's Cooking Tip

Ground moose is delicious—but it can also be very lean, depending on how much fat is added during the butchering process. If your moose meat is too dry, add some pork barrel belly fat from the governor's mansion. Yum!

THE MANY FACES OF SARAH PALIN

#5 Craig Ferguson was reportedly the first to comment on Sarah Palin's Sexy Librarian look.

Men seldom make passes at girls who wear glasses—or do they? It's one of the few things that Dorothy Parker was wrong about. Men just can't help themselves. When they see a "sexy librarian" type like Palin, they suffer an acid flashback to those bikini-clad dancers on David Lee Roth videos in the 1980s. Even if they were born in the 1990s.

Let's face it: It's a rare man-boy who can resist fantasizing about his hot school librarian. In Palin's case, she's burning up more than fantasy at the library. She's practically burning books.

Hmm. It actually sounds more like she's ready to ban anything not written by God.

BOOKED!

In 1996, Wasilla mayor Sarah Palin approached city librarian Mary Ellen Emmons and inquired how she might feel about censoring library books should she be asked to do so. As is often the case with these innocent-looking First Amendment radicals, Emmons reportedly retorted that she would definitely not condone the banning of any books. Within months, librarian Mary Ellen Emmons received a letter from Palin, telling her she was out (no word on the fate of the books). The censorship issue was not explicit; perhaps it amounted only to Dewey Decimal infractions. Nonetheless Palin felt Emmons didn't fully support her as mayor and so she had to go.

Well-liked and respected, Emmons had been a fixture at the library for seven years. After a public outcry, Palin changed her mind and let Emmons keep her job. She insists now that her book banning inquiry was simply "rhetorical."

DON'T JUDGE A BOOK BY HER COVER

Perhaps this sexy librarian look is Palin's revenge. She may look like a bookstack babe, but the Emmons affair begs the question: How would this VP handle issues of free speech? More important, maybe instead of exploring the banning of books, Palin should explore the reading of them.

TOP TEN BOOKS PALIN SHOULD READ
1. *An Inconvenient Truth* by Al Gore
2. *How to Talk so Teens Will Listen and Listen so Teens Will Talk* by Adele Faber and Elaine Mazlish
3. *Lipstick Jungle* by Candace Bushnell
4. *The Essential Feminist Reader* by Estelle Freeman
5. *The Audacity of Hope* by Barack Obama
6. *The Greens Cookbook* by Deborah Madison
7. *Fahrenheit 451* by Ray Bradbury
8. *Of Wolves and Men* by Barry Lopez
9. *A Brief History of Time* by Stephen Hawking
10. *The Travel Book: A Journey Through Every Country in the World* by Lonely Planet

Reports of the Monty Python/Sarah Palin connection are highly exaggerated.

Sarah Palin. Michael Palin. What besides last names do these two comedians share?

Michael Palin is one of the members of the well-known *Monty Python* comedy group, responsible for such classics as "The Dead Parrot."

Sarah Palin is one of the members of the well-known National Rifle Association, responsible for such classics as "the right to bear assault rifles in order to hunt defenseless deer."

One wonders whether there's some kind of "two great minds" vibe happening. Can we expect to see Secret Service agents clapping coconut halves together as they run alongside motorcades? Will future politicians sing about Spam as much as legislate it? Does Sarah Palin sing "The Lumberjack Song" as she thinks about oil development in the Arctic National Wildlife Refuge?

So many questions. But nobody expects answers.

#7 Sarah Palin has described herself as an "average hockey mom"—and proud of it.

Sarah Palin is a self-described "average hockey mom"—a play on the term "soccer mom" used by mothers like Palin up there in the Alaskan tundra. On the other hand, Palin says she is a "reformer" and seems to love referring to herself as a "pitbull." Like any politician, she is trying to play both sides of the fence. She wants to play the average hockey mom while also touting herself as a leader of men and women. We've seen this trick before. Unfortunately, politicians are all the same in this regard. It's hard to teach old pitbulls new tricks.

SARAH STAT

Despite the above differences between Pitbull Palin and other hockey moms, hockey mothers across the country are supporting Pailn. If you are one of them, get your "Hockey moms for Palin" T-shirts here: *www.cafepress.com/history2008*

HARDLY AN AVERAGE HOCKEY MOM

But under that pretty hockey mom exterior is a calculating politician out to win votes. Let's take a look at the average American hockey mom, as compared to Pitbull Palin.

Average Hockey Mom	Pitbull Palin
Reads a lot of books	Seeks to ban books
Meets most friends through the PTA	Meets most friends through the NRA
Drives an SUV around town	Drives a snowmobile with a mounted rifle
Watches *Maury Povich*	Hates Jews*
Makes breakfast for kids	Shoots breakfast for kids
Carpools kids around the suburbs	Snowmachines kids around the tundra
Lunches with the ladies	Dishes with the Elite Six
Plans family budget	Plans family hunts
Prays for world peace	Prays the gay away
Speaks in "Mom"	Speaks in tongues
Supports equal pay for equal work	Supports equal pork for equal oil

* Note: Palin's current church told the congregation that terrorist strikes against Israel are God's punishment of Jews for not accepting Jesus Christ. Palin still supports the church.

SARAH SAYS:

"You know what the difference is between a hockey mom and a pitbull? Lipstick."

—SARAH PALIN, AT THE 2008 REPUBLICAN
NATIONAL CONVENTION

Sarah Palin Is a VPILF!

Yes, just another of sexy Sarah's nicknames. VPILF is an acronym for Vice President I'd Like to F—k.* If you don't believe it, check out VPILF.com, a website dedicated to those who not only want to vote for Sarah Palin, but want to nail her as well.

There is no doubt that Palin is hot. She's red hot. She's a former beauty queen who hunts and loves sports. She's been known to fire anyone who crosses her path. She doesn't believe in evolution or sex education or libraries. What's not to like?

PALIN'S PERFECT DATE
If she were single, Palin's perfect date would probably be to go out into the woods and shoot some animals. Then, after skinning the animal and smearing blood on her hands and feet, the couple could go to church for a little Jesus time, then have

---

* VPILF is a variation of MILF, the acronym made famous in the guys-get-laid classic film *American Pie*. MILF stands for Mother I'd Like to F—k.

> [While looking at a picture of Stifler's mom]
> MILF Guy #2: Dude that chick's a MILF!
> MILF Guy #1: What to hell is that?
> MILF Guy #2: M-I-L-F Mom I'd Like to F**k!
> MILF Guy #1: Yeah dude! Yeah!
> (imdb.com)

a little candlelight moose dinner. And then it's to the bear-skin rug (homemade, of course) to cuddle and sip champagne. When things get hot, instead of tossing the glasses into the fireplace, they'd take any controversial literary classic and toss it into the flames. Be prepared, though—a good book burning is guaranteed to ignite the pitbull within.

OTHER VPILFS IN HISTORY

While Palin may have inspired the term, it shouldn't be restricted to women. There have been plenty of hot former VPs. Below is a list of the top 5.

Lyndon B. Johnson—he may not have been pretty, but rumor has it he had a really big . . . Johnson.

Dan Quayle—He was so stupid and nonthreatening, like a child who needs cuddling—and a spelling tutor.

Nelson Rockefeller—He was rich as hell.

Aaron Burr—Decent looking chap who knew how to use his gun—just ask Hamilton.

Al Gore—All that talk of global warming will no doubt get you hot.

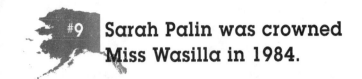

#9 Sarah Palin was crowned Miss Wasilla in 1984.

Sexy Sarah Palin began running for beauty pageants in order to win a scholarship to college (yes, they give scholarships for that). Palin won the Miss Wasilla Pageant in 1984, and then finished third (second runner-up) in the Miss Alaska pageant, indeed earning that college scholarship and the "Miss Congeniality" award (yes, they give Miss Congeniality awards to pitbulls).

Just so you know: The term beauty pageant has fallen out of favor with the half-naked girls parading down the runway sporting big hair, wide smiles, and high-heeled f—k-me pumps. They're called "achievement programs" now.

From the Miss America website:

> "I did lots of things. I was a pianist, but not quite good enough to get a music scholarship; an athlete, but I didn't play a varsity sport; smart, but not smart enough to get an academic scholarship. So competing in the Miss America program was an opportunity to get a scholarship for school."
>
> —Kellye Cash, Miss America 1987

WINNING BEAUTY PAGEANTS IN ALASKA
HINT: YOU'RE NOT IN TEXAS ANY MORE

Winning "achievement programs" in the Last Frontier is not the catwalk it is in the Lower 48. Should you be hankering for a crown—read: college scholarship—from Alaska, you should familiarize yourself with its quaint beauty customs.

Typical Beauty Pageant	Alaskan Beauty Pageant
Tiara	Snow mask
Line dancing	Snowmobiling
Baton-twirling	Skeet shooting*
Big hair	Big helmet hair
Sequins	Beaver fur
Satin sash	Rifle sling
Swimsuit competition	Long underwear competition
"World peace"	"Drill, baby, drill!"

* THE TALENT COMPETITION

Like all beauty pageants, the Miss Wasilla beauty pageant gives the lovely ladies a chance to showcase their special talents. In this competitive arena, Palin proved once again that she's not just another pretty face in a daring act that endeared her to Alaskans and Lower 48-ers alike. How many of you ladies out there can skin a bear cub while twirling a baton? Didn't think so.

Check out *www.digitalalchemy.tv/2008/08/miss-wasilla-photo-gallery-sarah-palin.html* to see a picture of Sarah in her beauty pageant days . . .

#10 **Sarah Palin was born under the sign of Aquarius—and astrologers say that's why she might be next vice president of the United States.**

SARAH PALIN: AQUARIUS FROM HELL?

Is this the dawning of the Age of Aquarius? According to astrologers, it's no accident that Sarah Palin, born February 11, 1964, while the sun was in the zodiac sign Aquarius, has suddenly burst onto the world scene. Some might even call it fate. If that's the case, we need to get to know Sarah better by considering some well-known Aquarian characteristics.

Aquarians Believe in Fairness. She'll show you fair: Sarah, mother of five, wants every woman to have an equal chance to experience the same joys of family life that she's been blessed with. Having an unwed, pregnant teenager in the house has also provided Sarah with valuable growth opportunities—that's why she's so strongly opposed to abortion.

Friendship Is Important to Aquarians. Palin is very, very, very friendly: As governor of Alaska, Sarah made lots of friends in the oil industry and the NRA. Now she's busy expanding her circle of friends in high places and will soon be on a first-name basis with every Washington lobbyist.

Aquarians Are Humanitarians. Sarah always puts people first, and don't you four-legged beasts forget it: Animal rights activists have criticized Sarah for allowing sport hunters to shoot bears and wolves from planes. However, these dangerous predators (the bears and wolves, that is) present potential hazards to humans and have been known to kill people. Sarah's support of aerial hunting clearly shows her concern for human rights and the safety of her fellow men/women.

Aquarians Love Excitement. Our Sarah's a regular adrenalin junkie: According to Kevin Drum of MotherJones.com, Sarah's willingness to go to war with Russia is not "something that Palin blurted out due to inexperience," which shows he understands that Sarah just likes to keep things interesting. What could be more exciting than a full-scale nuclear exchange?

Aquarians Are Idea People. Sarah's full of ideas, good, bad, and ugly: As mayor of Wasilla, Sarah demonstrated her keen interest in ideas and language when she sought to improve the quality of the local library by considering banning books that didn't meet her high standards.

Aquarians Like Trying New Things. She's the New Mom on the Block: After serving as mayor of the tiny city of Wasilla and briefly as governor of Alaska, with a population of only about 670,000, it's no surprise that Sarah is ready for something new. Her willingness to take on a huge challenge she's totally unprepared for demonstrates her Aquarian confidence and optimism.

CHANGE IS HERE TO STAY!

But here's the most important point to remember: Nobody loves change more than an Aquarian. And of course, change has always been a woman's prerogative.

#11 Sarah Palin and Sandra Bullock are one and the same Miss Congeniality. Does John McCain really want Sandra Bullock in a position of power outside of Hollywood?

THEY'RE BOTH FIRM AND INFLEXIBLE

According to *An Etymological Dictionary of Family and Christian Names with an Essay on their Derivation and Import*, the surname *Bullock* has the following meaning: "A full-grown ox. All the families of Bulls, Bullards, and Bullocks are noted for being firm and inflexible in their way." It's no coincidence, then, that Palin describes herself as being a pitbull with lipstick. And, in her own way, equally as firm and inflexible.

THEY SHARE THE SAME BIRTHYEAR

Both women were born in 1964. Oh, sure, Bullock was "supposedly" born in July and Palin in February, but that little smokescreen isn't fooling anyone.

THEY WERE BOTH "MISS CONGENIALITIES"

Sarah Palin was named Miss Congeniality in the 1984 Miss Alaska Pageant. She is also a member of the NRA and carries a gun. Sandra Bullock starred in the film *Miss Congeniality* in 2000 (not coincidentally, the same year George W. Bush was elected president). In the movie, she plays a federal agent posing as a flag-waving beauty pageant contestant. Throughout, she wears a gun strapped to her thigh—just like the Sarah Palin action figure detailed in entry #72! In addition, the title of the sequel, *Miss Congeniality 2: Armed & Fabulous*, reads as if it was specifically meant to describe Governor Palin. (Do you see how all this comes together?)

THEY HAVE (OR ARE ABOUT TO HAVE) CONNECTIONS TO THE PENTAGON

Sandra Bullock's father was a Pentagon contractor. Sarah may soon be spending a lot of time in that very same building. Coincidence? Doubtful. Given that the two women are one and the same, there can be no question that Bullock's father helped orchestrate her rise to power. The real question is: What dirt does John Bullock have on John McCain? Hmm.

BOTH WERE HIGH SCHOOL ATHLETES

Bullock attended Washington-Lee High School, where she was a cheerleader. Palin may soon reside in Washington, and though she isn't a cheerleader, she would be serving underneath a former high school athlete and was an athlete herself. It's a familiar story . . .

THEY HAVE NEVER BEEN SEEN TOGETHER

Sandra Bullock and Sarah Palin are never seen together—because they can't be. Take off those glasses, Governor Palin! It might have worked for Superman, but it won't work for you!

Sarah Palin once dressed as Tina Fey for Halloween. She gained 20 IQ points and a sense of humor.

Tina Fey returned the favor when she donned her signature specs and an updo and nailed Palin in a scathingly funny *SNL* season-opening skit. Let's look at how these women stack up:

FEY: Wrote and anchored *SNL*'s Weekend Update, a faux look at the news, for four years
PALIN: Worked as a sports reporter for KTUU-TV in Anchorage, Alaska, for five minutes

FEY: Topped numerous hot lists, including *Time*, *People*, and *Maxim* magazines; also placed seventh on that 2007 Hot 100 List on AfterEllen.com, a website for lesbian women
PALIN: Featured in *Vogue*'s "Governor Issue" as "New Faces to Watch in 2008"; high on neoconservatives' lists of hotties

FEY: Greek Orthodox
PALIN: "Bible-believing" Christian who believes war in Iraq is "God's plan"

FEY: Committed environmentalist; drives a hybrid
PALIN: Committed to ruining the environment; wants to knock polar bears off the endangered species list

FEY: Gave birth for the first time at age thirty-five
PALIN: Gave birth for the first time at age twenty-five, then had her fifth child at age forty-four, and no end in sight

Part 2

THE EARLY YEARS

#13 Sarah Louise Heath was born in Idaho, not Alaska. (Not that there's much difference to the naked eye. Both are short on people and long on winter.)

Sandpoint, population 6,835, is where little Sarah began the journey that would take her from the northern Idaho country once home to the Aryan Nations to (God willing) the White House, now home to the lamest president in U.S. history.

Other famous people who call Sandpoint home include:

★ Cop Mark Fuhrman, of O.J. Simpson trial fame
★ Football great Jerry Kramer, former Green Bay Packers right guard
★ Outfielder Joe Mather of the St. Louis Cardinals
★ Actors Ben Stein and Viggo Mortensen
★ Writers Patrick F. McManus and Marilynne Robinson

According to the Sandpoint Chamber of Commerce:
"Nestled between the rugged Selkirk and Cabinet Mountains is a quaint historical town called Sandpoint, Idaho boasting a first-class ski resort, Schweitzer Mountain Resort, and the largest lake in Idaho, Lake Pend Oreille."

Why would anyone leave such a lovely place, you ask? Why, only to move to Wasilla, of course!

THE SANDPOINT, IDAHO, MOTTO: "WORK HARD. PLAY HARDER."

Sarah Palin obviously has taken that motto to heart:

Work Hard: Run for governor
Play Harder: Run for vice president
Work Hard: Tie your hair up in a bun for Democrats
Play Harder: Let your hair down for Republicans
Work Hard: Support hard-line Republican issues
Play Harder: Run with maverick McCain
Work Hard: Fight like a pitbull on the campaign trail
Play Harder: Make pitbull jokes at the RNC
Work Hard: Wear the pants in Alaska
Play Harder: Wear pencil skirts in the Lower 48

YOU MIGHT BE FROM IDAHO IF YOU:

★ Eat potatoes more than three times a day.
★ Can make French-fried potatoes forty-seven different ways.
★ Are sick to death of potatoes.
★ Know your jasper from your jade.
★ Can recite cowboy poetry by heart.
★ Think cowboy poetry is poetry.

SARAH STAT

Coldwater Creek, the women's retailer known for its uninspired (read: frumpy) clothing for middle-aged women, is headquartered in Sandpoint. Perhaps all those fashionistas debating where the once-racy Sarah buys her clothes now that she's the VP candidate should look closer to home.

#14 Sally and Charlie Heath moved their family to Alaska when Sarah was an infant.

If you're like most Americans, you've never been to Alaska or Idaho. So you may not know how very different they are. Let us educate you:

★ Idaho is cold, Alaska is colder.
★ Idaho is big, Alaska is bigger.
★ Idaho has relatively few people, Alaska has even fewer.
★ Idaho's highest point is Borah Peak at 12,662 ft., Alaska's highest point is Mt. McKinley at 20,320 ft.
★ Idaho has seven national parks and historic trails, Alaska has fifteen.

Enough. Let's face it: Idaho is the poor man's Alaska. No wonder the Heaths went North to the Future!

SARAH STAT

"North to the Future" is the Alaskan state motto. Of course, now Governor Palin is heading south to her future. Just don't tell the Alaskans.

WORDS YOU SHOULD KNOW IN ALASKA

Word	Definition
Alaskan Horse	The biggest mosquitoes you have ever seen in your non-Alaskan life.
Blue Cloud	A clearing in the clouds. Sort of.
Breakup	When the ice melts and the rivers flow, and winter finally, finally, finally ends.
The Bush	No, not George W. It's the part of Alaska inaccessible by road . . . which used to be most of it, until global warming.
Bush Pilot	A pilot who flies around the bush in a small plane outfitted with floats or skis. Think First Dude.
Cabin Fever	The reason Alaskans go stark raving mad every year.
Calve	When ice breaks off from a glacier to form icebergs, it calves. Think global warming.
Cheechako	If you're new to Alaska, you're a cheechako. Watch your step.
Chum	Dog salmon.
Iditarod	The annual thousand-mile sled dog race from Anchorage to Nome.
Iron Dog Race	Same as above, only longer and with snowmobiles instead of dog sleds. Think First Dude, again.
Lower 48	What locals call the continental U.S.
Mukluks	The sealskin or reindeer-skin boots preferred by the Inuit.
Outside	Anywhere but Alaska. I'm talking to you, cheechako.
Pay Dirt	Placer gold that means big money for miners.
Quiviut	Alaskan musk ox wool.
Southeast	Southeast Alaska.
Sourdough	Old-timer—or anyone who's survived a winter in Alaska.
Taku Wind	100-mile-per-hour winds that make rain fall sideways. Sideways!
Termination Dust	The first snow of the winter.
Ulu	Knife shaped like a fan used to cut caribou and other meat.

#15 As the third of four children, Sarah Palin is considered a middle child. And you know what that means.

As the classic middle child, Sarah is by definition:
Rebellious—she thumbed her nose at old-school Republicans, all the way to the VP nomination
Fierce—they don't call her Sarah Barracuda for nothing
A good negotiator—playing chicken with the oil companies in Alaska
Competitive—she took on long-time incumbent Gov. Frank Murkowski and won, becoming the youngest governor and the first female governor in Alaska history
More likely to engage in dangerous sports—snowmobiling, moose hunting, presidential politics

OTHER MIDDLES
Sarah's in good company with other middle children, such as:

★ Donald Trump
★ Ted Kennedy
★ Julia Roberts
★ Bill Gates
★ J.F.K.
★ Madonna
★ Princess Diana

SARAH STAT

Sarah Palin has three siblings . . . but they're not talking. Never mess with a middle child.

THE EARLY YEARS

#16 When Sarah Palin was a little girl, her father, Charlie, reportedly often took her moose hunting before school.

Wow. It's so nice when a father spends quality time with his kids. And even better when that quality time provides not only fun, but breakfast as well. We can only imagine what other sorts of exciting and educational activities this happy father and daughter might have shared:

* Baby Beaver Butchery
* Seal Cub Clubbing
* Teddy Bear Trapping
* Puppy Dog Drowning
* Bambi Bullet Bingo
* Rubber Ducky Roulette
* Kitty Cat Kill
* Elk Calf Carnage

CHARLIE HEATH'S MOOSE
HUNTING TIPS FOR KIDS
* Always wear orange.
* Carry your gun upright, like a baton.
* Keep your finger off the trigger until you are ready to kill.
* Never point your gun at Daddy.

> **SARAH STAT**
>
> There's a gun in 50 percent of all U.S. households, according to the NRA.

Spicy Sausage and Moose
Breakfast Casserole

Serves 8-10

If your butcher makes game breakfast sausage, then use it for this recipe. Or use ground moose and spice it up with fennel, red pepper flakes, and assorted herbs like oregano and basil. This casserole is easy to assemble at the last minute and holds well on a buffet. Add homemade biscuits and moose gravy, it's a feast your whole family will love! Perfect for a big post-hunt brunch!

½ pound ground moose

½ pound spicy breakfast sausage

Kosher salt and freshly ground pepper to taste

2 (4-ounce) cans green chilies, chopped

1 cup Monterey jack cheese, shredded

12 eggs

1½ cups whole milk

Salsa, sour cream, and chopped green onions

1. Preheat oven to 350°F. Grease a large baking dish and set aside.
2. Brown meat and place evenly in the baking dish. Season to taste with salt and pepper. Sprinkle green chilies, then cheese, evenly over meat.
3. With the back of a spoon, slightly hollow 12 places for the eggs (away from the edge of the baking dish). Break eggs into the indentations and lightly break yolks with a fork. Pour milk over all and bake for about 30 to 40 minutes, just until set.
4. Serve with salsa, sour cream, and chopped green onions on the side.

#17 Sarah Palin's father, Charlie Heath, is a retired science teacher and track coach.

When you remember that Sarah Palin strongly supports the teaching of creationism in schools, you have to wonder exactly what kind of science teacher Mr. Heath was.

It's the obvious: He was an evangelical Christian science teacher. But before you can say "oxymoron," let's take a closer look at the man and his God and his science.

DADDY WAS A TEACHER MAN

Aside from the obvious inconvenience that he will know that the sled dog did not eat your homework, having a science teacher for a dad has other challenges. Charlie taught science and cross-country running; one of his students was his own daughter. Surely she benefited from studying both disciplines. All that dissection in science lab comes in handy for any hunter. (Years before the controversy about what happens when you put lipstick on it, there were fetal pigs to be cut, long thermometers, and glass vials of both innocuous and caustic liquids.) And running is an essential skill, whether you're blowing up Bunsen burners, outpacing a bear in the Alaskan wild, or fighting scandalous rumors in the press.

THINKING OUTSIDE THE CLASSROOM

Palin's parents initially raised their daughter Roman Catholic, and then upon their move to Alaska affiliated themselves

SARAH SAYS:

"Teach both [creationism and evolution]. You know, don't be afraid of information. . . . Healthy debate is so important and it's so valuable in our schools. I am a proponent of teaching both. And you know, I say this too as the daughter of a science teacher. Growing up with being so privileged and blessed to be given a lot of information on, on both sides of the subject—creationism and evolution. It's been a healthy foundation for me. But don't be afraid of information and let kids debate both sides."

—SARAH PALIN

with the Wasilla Assembly of God, a Pentecostal church. The schism between what we learn in tattered schoolbooks at high marble-topped stations and in the Bible is considerable. The timeline of millions of years versus several thousand alone is something to consider.

A textbook and the Good Book are not good dance partners. All that geology and carbon-dating awe us when we hold a fossil in our hands or behold some ancient geologic formation. We look at the old bones, evidence that shows us dinosaurs roamed the earth long before modern man or tenacious insurance agents.

How, then, to reconcile those old dinosaur bones with creationism? We all know the folks who pull that ultimate faith trigger, like our dear Aunt Blanchie: "I know there were no dinosaurs because they were not mentioned in the Bible!"

But Charlie is no Aunt Blanchie. He's a science teacher. But obviously one with a capacity for contemplating paradox.

WHO BELIEVES WHAT—AND THAT MEANS YOU

Which of the following statements most accurately describes your attitude toward the beginning of time and man?

1. God created human beings pretty much in their present form at one time within the last 10,000 years or so.
2. Human beings have developed over millions of years from less advanced forms of life, but God guided this process.
3. Human beings have developed over millions of years from less advanced forms of life, but God had no part in this process.

If you answered number one, you are a creationist. Choose number two, and you're a theist. Number three means you're a naturalist and are probably going straight to hell.

Gallup started asking Americans to identify themselves as one of these believers (or nonbelievers) back in 1982 and have continued to do so. The numbers have remained fairly constant:

Creationists: 44 to 47 percent
Theists: 35 to 40 percent
Naturalists: 9 to 13 percent

Which means either Charlie Heath is in the minority—or we need better science teachers.

WHO BELIEVES IN CREATIONISM, BY PARTY
73 percent of Republicans
58 percent of Democrats
57 percent of Independents

Source: 2005 Harris poll

SARAH STAT

According to Gallup, only 5 percent of scientists believe in creationism.

WHO BELIEVES IN CREATIONISM, BY REGION
Americans living in the Northeast and West are much less likely to believe in creationism than those in the South and Midwest. *Note:* Apparently Alaska is its own region, which may explain everything.

WHO BELIEVES IN CREATIONISM, BY AGE

Americans fifty-five and older are much more likely to believe in creationism than those under fifty-five. Which explains our Aunt Blanchie.

WHO BELIEVES IN CREATIONISM, BY EDUCATION AND INCOME

College students are half as likely to believe in creationism as people without a high school education. Americans who earn more than $50,000 per year are half as likely to believe in creationism as those who earn less than $20,000.

Source: Gallup

AROUND THE WORLD CREATED BY GOD IN SEVEN DAYS—OR NOT

In 2006, *Science* magazine conducted a study of global attitudes toward evolution, polling thirty-four countries. Turkey aside, the United States came in last in terms of an accepting attitude toward evolution. Nearly 40 percent of Americans rejected evolution outright, compared to only 7 to 15 percent in Europe and Japan.

And we wonder why our kids are so far behind in math and science compared to other developed countries.

#18 Sarah Palin has admitted that she smoked marijuana as a teenager, albeit at a time when Alaska had decriminalized use of the drug.

HALF-BAKED ALASKA

She may look like a librarian, but don't let that bun and those spectacles fool you. Sarah Palin (aka Mary Jane) is a pothead—or was. She admits to smoking dope when she was younger. But as her campaign rightfully points out, it was legal at the time in the state of Alaska.

We're beginning to understand why people would live in that state.

REEFER MCCAIN MADNESS

Palin claims that while she did inhale, she didn't like it. *Riiight.* But are these excuses good enough for McCain or his conservative followers? McCain is an advocate for the federal prosecution of medical marijuana patients and providers who operate legally under California law. So our savvy Sarah now supports legislation that calls for the arrest of other people who smoke marijuana, even though she

SARAH STAT

Alaska still has the country's most lenient marijuana laws, allowing an adult to possess up to one ounce of pot at home. Over four ounces is a felony, however—if admittedly a pretty darn good high.

wasn't arrested for doing the same thing. Spoilsport.

POTTY POOPER

Palin now opposes the legalization of pot because of the "message" it would send to her children. We actually buy this, since her kids are reportedly in enough trouble as it is.

TOP TEN REASONS TO
GET STONED IN ALASKA

1. You're stuck on an ice flow
2. You're stuck on the Bridge to Nowhere
3. You're stuck on an Alaskan cruise
4. Sarah Palin is your mayor
5. Sarah Palin is your governor
6. Sarah Palin is your president
7. You're in Alaska
8. You're lost in Alaska
9. You live in Alaska
10. You're gonna die in Alaska.

SARAH SAYS:

"I can't claim a Bill Clinton and say that I never inhaled."

—SARAH PALIN

SARAH'S FAVORITE MARY JANE MUNCHIE

When Sarah Palin gets stoned, like everyone else, she gets the munchies. But she solves the problem in a big way, Alaskan style. Here's the supersnack she whips up to quash the munchies when she and her Elite Six pals are getting blazed.

Blazing Big Sky
Killer Elk Chili

Serves
6-8

If you're short on elk, you can substitute any big game—buffalo, deer, moose, antelope, and bear all work well with this chili. If this recipe makes more than you need, it freezes well.

2 cups dried pinto beans, soaked overnight

3 pounds ground elk

2 onions, chopped

3 cloves garlic, minced

1 (28-ounce) can fire-roasted tomatoes

2 tablespoons cider vinegar

1 chipotle pepper from a can of chipotle peppers in adobo sauce

1 teaspoon adobo sauce

3 tablespoons chili powder

1 tablespoon ground cumin

Kosher salt and freshly ground black pepper to taste

2 cups sharp Cheddar cheese, shredded

1 red onion, diced

1 cup mixed fresh herbs, chopped (parsley, cilantro, and chives)

1. After soaking overnight, rinse beans well and set aside.
2. Brown meat in a large pot over medium-high heat. Add onions and garlic and cook until soft, about 7 to 8 minutes. Add can of tomatoes and cider vinegar.
3. Finely chop the chipotle pepper and add to the pot. Add adobo sauce, chili powder, and cumin and season with salt and pepper to taste. Stir well and bring to a boil. Add 2 or 3 cups of water if chili is too thick; readjust seasonings. Turn heat down to a simmer and cover. Cook for 30 minutes or longer.
4. Set cheese, red onion, and herbs in separate bowls for garnishing. Then serve chili.

Sarah's Cooking Tip: Chipotle Peppers in Adobo Sauce

This is a marvelously smooth and hot product. The only problem is it's an 11-ounce can filled with 10 or 12 chipotle peppers and almost ½ cup adobo sauce. Most recipes call for only 1 or 2 peppers, no matter how stoned you are. Place the peppers on parchment paper on a tray and freeze them individually so the rest of the can does not go to waste.

#19 Sarah Palin was born in 1964, a year remarkably similar to 2008.

1964 was a watershed year: The Beatles came to America; antiwar activists marched in a major demonstration against the Vietnam War; President Lyndon Johnson signed the Civil Rights Act; the biggest earthquake in U.S. history struck Anchorage, Alaska; and Sarah Louise Heath was born in Sandpoint, Idaho.

Coincidence? We think not.

1964	2008
Vietnam War	Iraq and Afghanistan Wars
War on Poverty	War on the Middle Class
Ford Mustang debuts	Ford Roush Mustang debuts
Jack Ruby convicted	Saddam Hussein convicted
Summer Olympics held in Tokyo	Summer Olympics held in Beijing
Warren Commission published	*101 Things You—and John McCain—Didn't Know about Sarah Palin* published
Martin Luther King, Jr. wins Nobel Peace Prize	Al Gore wins Nobel Peace Prize

The more things change, the more they stay the same.

Part 3
ENTER THE
FIRST DUDE

#20 Sarah Heath and Todd Palin were high school sweethearts in Wasilla, Alaska.

Sarah and Todd dated through high school. Years later, August 29, 1988, they happily chose to unite legally. Unfortunately, they also described their finances at the time as a "bad year of fishing." No, we didn't make that up. You can't make that s—t up. *Note:* When Ivana Trump used those very words when accepting the Donald's proposal, she had another type of fishing in mind.

THE GOLDEN CHURLS

The inexpensive $35 process fee for elopement was attractive. So they approached the Palmer, Alaska, courthouse, only to find that they were short the two witnesses required by law. They improvised, and reportedly brought in two residents of a nearby nursing home as witnesses. Rumors that they chose convalesced witnesses in case of the need for a coverup on the nuptials are quite overstated. Time has proven the marriage to be long-lasting, like the ubiquitous red Jello at a hospital cafeteria, or, well, a retirement home.

Which reminds us of a joke: A justice of the peace was called to a nursing home to perform a wedding. He was led to an old man down the corridor in his suite. The bride-to-be was still on her way, so the justice sat down to ask the old man a few questions.

"This must be a special woman."

"I guess I like her," replied the old gentleman.

"Is she a good woman?"

"I don't know for sure," the resident answered.

"Does she have lots of money?" asked the JP.

"I doubt it."

"Then why are you marrying her?"

"She can drive at night," the old man said.

GET ME TO THE CRUTCH ON TIME

We all do what we have to for love and locomotion. When looking at any couple, it may prove hard to tell just who is doing the driving. Whether it's the First Dude or Sarah Barracuda in their marriage—well, the only witnesses are most likely dead and gone by now.

TOP TEN REASONS TO ELOPE

1. You're broke.
2. She's pregnant.
3. Her mother hates you.
4. Your mother hates her.
5. Her father has a shotgun.
6. It's your thirty-seventh wedding.
7. You promised you'd wait until you got married to have sex—and you're done waiting.
8. You really, really, really need a green card.
9. Her ninety-day fiancée visa expires tomorrow.
10. You love each other so much you can't wait another day.

First Dude and active outdoorsman Todd Palin has won the Tesoro Iron Dog snowmobile race four times.

Such honors are rarely typical of First Dudes and Dudettes. Laura Bush likes to read books, Lynne Cheney likes to write them (lesbian romance novels, in fact). The spouses of presidents and vice presidents are seldom known as vigorous sports enthusiasts. Okay, Tipper Gore played the drums to blow off stream, but that doesn't count as an actual sport. That precedent may well change if Todd Palin comes to town as the consort of the vice president.

As a champion racer, fisherman, and hunter, Todd Palin is clearly your quintessential All-American sportsman. Rugged. Quiet. Chiseled jaw. You know the type.

Has there ever been anyone in the presidential circle quite like him? Yes, there has.

And her name was Jackie.

TAME THE WILD BEAST

Oh? Yes. Jackie Kennedy was perfectly at home astride a huge beast, competing in the countryside for trophies and ribbons. She rode a horse; Palin rides a gas-guzzling snowmobile, but they are both driven to win and end up in the front of the pack at all costs. And win Jackie did. Known as a fierce competitor with a steely demeanor, she sat tall on her steed and rode through the Virginia countryside on local hunts. Todd was tossed from his seat and broke an arm in his latest race; Jackie was tossed off her horse on a jump and broke an arm.

Could Todd Palin bring his snowmobile to Washington and ride along those same country paths? Interesting idea. He'd have to clear it with the Master of the Foxhounds first, and also swap his down coat for a little pink hacking jacket. Tallyho, Todd!

TOP TEN SPORTS FOR FIRST DUDES
AND FIRST DUDETTES
1. Tea-Pouring Marathon
2. Fashion Fun Ski Run
3. Stand by Your Man/Woman Sparring
4. Shooting the Bulls—t Gallery
5. Smile Till You Drop Endurance Test
6. Ride Your Opponent Rodeo
7. Etiquette Boot Camp
8. Fundraising Fox Hunt
9. Diplomacy Dressage
10. Get the Vote Out Telethon

POLITICS IS NO LAUGHING MATTER
"I like Sarah Palin; she looks like the dip sample lady at Safeway."

—DAVE LETTERMAN

#22 Sarah Palin allegedly had an affair with her husband's former business partner in the mid-1990s.

According to dekerivers.wordpress.com: "Palin's husband Todd owned a snowmobile dealership with his business partner Brad Hanson. Apparently, Hanson, who was also married, and Sarah got on famously; Alaskan Abroad's sources say the two were 'flirtatious but never consummated the relationship.'"

Well, something happened. Because when Todd became aware of whatever was happening, he reportedly dissolved the partnership and sold the dealership. Hanson now serves on the Palmer City Council.

Did the First Dude overact—or was there really something going on between Hanson and Palin? Maybe it was nothing more than a flirtation. Maybe it was more, and Todd and Sarah worked it out. Or maybe running a snowmobile dealership just sucks.

The McCain campaign has gone on record as saying the "affair story" is nothing more than a "vicious lie."

It seems the nature of all political candidates, and particularly the conservative Republican stock, to maintain a marriage-etched-in-granite appearance. Time will tell.

TOP TEN SIGNS YOUR REPUBLICAN VICE
PRESIDENTIAL NOMINEE WIFE MAY BE
HAVING AN AFFAIR

1. She seems distracted rather than charmed when you use
   your "pull this lever" joke.
2. She asks McCain about extra rooms at the White House.
3. You catch her on the phone to Bill Clinton—asking him
   about discreet hiding places in the oval office.
4. She's Windexing her glasses more often.
5. You find a third set of snowmobile tracks in the side yard.
6. She starts using the word "caucus" more than usual.
7. She glares at you through the window while chopping
   wood.
8. You discover unfamiliar snowshoes under the bed.
9. She giggles when you say, "I'm gonna put on my rub-
   bers and go outside."
10. There's an elephant in the bedroom.

SARAH SAYS:

*"Throw in his Yupik Eskimo ancestry,
and it all makes for quite a
package. We met in high school, and
two decades and five children later he's
still my guy."*

—SARAH PALIN, ON HER HUSBAND TODD PALIN

#23 Sarah Palin and First Dude Todd have close ties to the Alaskan Independence Party. Known for seeking to secede from the United States.

No matter how much they try to hide it, Sarah Palin and her hubby Todd can't shake the fact that they have courted the Alaskan Independent Party (AIP) for many years. Todd himself was a member from 1995–2002 (with a brief hiatus in 2000). As for Sarah, she addressed the Party's convention in 2000, and again in 2008 as well.

ALASKA FIRST—ALASKA ALWAYS

That's the motto of the Alaskan Independent Party—a far, far weirder cry than the "Country First" motto of the McCain/Palin ticket. In fact, Joe Vogler, founder of the controversial party that has sought to secede from the Union since its inception, was no fan of our nation. Indeed, he stated in one interview that, "The fires of hell are frozen glaciers compared to my hatred for the American government." He also insisted that he "…won't be buried under their damn flag."

Their flag?

Hmm, we wonder what the reaction would be if Barack Obama were closely associated with someone spouting such anti-American sentiments. Just a thought . . .

ENTER THE FIRST DUDE

DEFINE TREASON

"I swear to protect and defend the Constitution of the United States from all enemies foreign and domestic."

That is part of an oath that Sarah Palin swore to uphold when she became governor of Alaska. So why isn't it treason to attend conventions of a political party who wants to secede? Oh, that's right. It's not treason if you're a hockey mom who loves Jesus.

From the Alaskan Independence Party's website:

The Alaskan Independence Party's goal is the vote we were entitled to in 1958, one choice from among the following four alternatives:

1. *Remain a Territory.*
2. *Become a separate and Independent Nation.*
3. *Accept Commonwealth status.*
4. *Become a State.*

The call for this vote is in furtherance of the dream of the Alaskan Independence Party's founding father, Joe Vogler, which was for Alaskans to achieve independence under a minimal government, fully responsive to the people, promoting a peaceful and lawful means of resolving differences.

SARAH STAT

Chairman of the AIP Lynette Clark told *ABC News* that both Sarah and Todd Palin were members in 1994. Ms. Clark was AIP secretary at the time.

TOP TEN REASONS WHY ALASKA MIGHT WANT TO SECEDE FROM THE UNION

1. Guilt over pocketing the dough for the Bridge to Nowhere.
2. In Alaska, nowhere is somewhere.
3. Pissed that their fellow Americans often forget Alaska is a state during geography car games.
4. Pathetic play for attention.
5. It's something to do.
6. Plan to invade Canada.
7. Jealous that Hawaii was last to join the Union.
8. Feels U.S. is overrun by Puerto Ricans.
9. Suffering from Seasonal Affective Disorder.
10. Want to legalize marijuana, again.

TOP TEN REASONS WE WANT TO KEEP ALASKA

1. One word: Oil.
2. Two words: Natural gas.
3. With Alaska, we're still bigger than China.
4. With Alaska, we're still bigger than Brazil.
5. Unlimited access to mukluks.
6. First dibs on Alaskan king crab.
7. With global warming, it'll become the new Sun City.
8. *Deadliest Catch* is the coolest show on cable.
9. Nostalgia for TV show *Northern Exposure*.
10. Because we can.

ENTER THE FIRST DUDE

24

The happy couple celebrated their twentieth wedding anniversary on the very day Sarah Palin was announced as McCain's pick.

The scene went a little something like this:

Sarah: "Baby, you gonna put me on the back of that snowmobile tonight?"
Todd: "I'm tired from taking care of the baby . . ."
Sarah: "I'm drunk on power, isn't this hot?"
Todd: "I'm drunk on this Kool-Aid you've been serving up . . ."
Sarah: "Honey, let's make another baby!"
Todd: "Whatever you say, governor . . . "

THE BACKSTORY
The pair met when Todd transferred to Sarah Heath's high school and they met at a basketball game. It was love at first sight. (He grew up salmon fishing, but always loved exotic fish, you see.) Immediately enamored with her marksmanship and predatorlike qualities, Todd and Barracuda became an item.

That's how they roll in Alaska. Although a pickup truck makes more sense in the wilds of the Last Frontier, a picture has surfaced of Sarah as a high-school senior with fabulous feathered hair, posing in front of the future First Dude's sporty Ford Mustang. (It's a good thing they were both svelte and athletic; that model's back seat is so small, it's tough to get it on!)

After graduation, our girl's college and beauty queen ambitions seemed to take their toll on poor Todd, who was left back in Alaska drinking and shooting things up with his buddies (he was brought up on drunk driving charges in 1986). Tired of "abstinence," in 1988, he finally reportedly knocked Sarah up, er . . . convinced her to marry, and the couple eloped. "We had a bad fishing year that year, so we didn't have any money," Todd said. "So we decided to spend 35 bucks and go down to the courthouse." Fewer than eight months later, the happy couple welcomed their first son Track.

These days, the First Dude's ambition has come to match his better half's. As fierce Iron Dog champion, Todd's racing partner claims, "You know, I think this is the longest I've been partners with anybody."

Barracuda, you might want to watch your back.

SARAH SAYS:

"He [Todd] can go on just an hour or two of sleep a night. He says, 'I can sleep when I die.' There is no way I could have done this job without his tremendous contributions to the home life."

—SARAH PALIN,
IN "TODD PALIN UNIQUE AMONG NATION'S 5 FIRST HUSBANDS" BY JEANNETTE J. LEE, ADN.COM, 5/27/2007.

25

Sarah Palin has the hottest spouse in politics since Jackie.

Todd Palin, known affectionately to Alaskans as the "First Dude" (a nickname that he also calls himself), is loved by the people of his state. After all, he is one of them, a blue-collar college dropout who has spent his professional life working hard with his hands in the oil fields of Alaska and as a fisherman. He has earned respect as a champion snowmobile racer, a talent Alaskans revere second only to shooting animals.

"I have to trust my life in his hands, and I do," his racing partner Scott Davis said. "A lot of teams certainly don't have fun when they're doing it, and I like to think Todd and I do."

But he is also popular because he is hot. Red hot. He is so damn hot he could set a glacier on fire. Just picturing him lying on a bed wearing only snowshoes and his award-winning smile is enough to turn even the most conservative God-loving Pentecostal Christian into a sexually charged hellcat. Right, Sarah?

TOP TEN REASONS WHY THE FIRST DUDE IS HOT

1. Decades of digging in Alaska's oil and gas fields have turned his body into a well-oiled machine.
2. He looks good in camouflage.
3. He apparently held his own at tea party for former First Ladies of Alaska—and they're a notoriously intellectual bunch.

4. He compensates for being a moron by f—king really, really, well.
5. They call him "Alaskan King Cock."
6. He is one-eighth Native Alaskan. How many of us can say we've f—ked an Eskimo?
7. He isn't *too* smart.
8. They call his abs the "Lower 48."
9. He can ride a snowmobile really fast.
10. He's hung like a moose.

FIRST DUDE'S IDEAL FIRST DATE

He'll pick you up about eight, which in the rest of the country looks like high noon, put you on the back of his Harley snowmobile and race you around town, your hair blowing in the wind. Remember to hold on tight to him just as he likes—*real* tight; he crashed his snowmobile last February during a race and went flying 70 feet.

After that, it's time to catch something to eat. Don't worry, if you're not into it, he won't make you eat the still-beating heart of the beast that pumps in his blood-ridden hand.

And then the romance *really* kicks off. Time for some beer at the old sports bar. A couple of pints of those and it's back on the snowmobile, only this time he'll be making doughnuts in the snow and joking about how if you fell off in the middle of nowhere you might die without a soul knowing where you are.

Finally, if you're lucky, a good ol' roll in the snow stack awaits you. Buckle up.

It's going to be a wild ride!

26

First Dude Todd Palin is one of wife Sarah Palin's top budget advisers.

Todd Palin is Alaska's Renaissance man. Ladies, this guy's got it all! He's a loving dad to five kids! He's a rugged outdoorsman who loves to hunt and fish! He's a hardworking steelworker! He's married to the Guv-Babe! He's an unofficial advisor to her administration, especially on her budget work! Huh?

Which of these things is not like the others?

CREATIVE ACCOUNTING, WASILLA STYLE

A guy who has "taken some college classes but never received a degree" is one of the 'Cuda's major budget advisors? Isn't that sort of like having an accountant whose only real "education" with numbers is balancing his own checkbook? Remember, folks, this guy's been married for twenty years. Do you really think he's handled any of the family money any time since Reagan was president? If he's like every other husband in America—no way.

Think maybe Todd was the one who came up with the bright idea of having the 'Cuda charge the state of Alaska per diem (to the tune of $17,000!) for nights spent in her own home? Now that's what we call creative accounting.

First Stud Todd is Sarah Palin's Nancy Reagan. Insiders claim that he's involved in virtually every decision Palin makes—which may have led him into hot water. He's apparently elbow-deep in the mess rapidly spinning out of the McCain campaign's ability to spin it known as "Troopergate" (see page 92 for more on this dizzy little affair). Yep, the First Fisherman has been cc'ed on nearly every e-mail exchange between the 'Cuda, her staff, and Walt Monegan, the guy she reportedly fired for not firing her ex-bro-in-law.

Todd Palin has allegedly had several conversations with Monegan where he's gone on record asking Monegan to fire his ex-brother-in-law. Note: He's obviously been privy to the ex-brother-in-law's confidential service record, having referenced a number of aspects of the record of the trooper in question that are supposed to be "confidential."

BANKING ON 2008
Imagine what he could do as "First Dude" of the Nation! Who needs a budget director on staff when Todd is acting as an "unpaid advisor"?

Part 4

FAMILY FIRST
(OR NOT)

#27 **Sarah Palin has made it clear that her kids should be above media scrutiny during the campaign— and most everyone, including her opponents, agrees with her.**

That said, parading your cute kids around on stage in the hope of impressing the voters with your "family values" and then asking everyone to take no notice of them when they are revealed (surprise, surprise!) as not quite perfect simply smacks of politics as usual.

Inevitably, the families of politicians are thrust into the spotlight, examined from every angle, and ultimately tossed on the table in a bidding war for the media's attention. And whether they like to admit it or not, these parental pols raise the stakes and bet the family farm and all its occupants, willing or unwilling, every time they play another round of presidential poker.

SARAH SAYS:

"We ask the media to respect our daughter and Levi's privacy as has always been the tradition of children of candidates."

—SARAH AND TODD PALIN

In the race for vice president, the cards stack up like this:

- *Sarah Palin's son, Track, is being deployed to Iraq.* Plus.
- *Joseph Biden's son, Beau, is being deployed to Iraq.* Plus.

- *Sarah Palin's seventeen-year-old daughter is pregnant.* Okay.
- *Joseph Biden's son, Hunter, is a lawyer.* Okay.

- *Joseph Biden lost his first wife and young daughter in a car crash at Christmastime. His boys were injured, and he nursed them back to health. Five years later, he married again, and with second wife Jill, he had his daughter Ashley.* God bless them all.
- *Sarah Palin gave birth at forty-four to Trig, an infant with Down syndrome. Knowing this, she and her husband chose to continue the pregnancy.* God bless them all.

- *Sarah Palin also has two more children, daughters Willow and Piper.* Plus. Plus.

Five aces trumps three any time. In this political game as well as every other, Sarah Palin proves that she can afford to play high-stakes poker. After all, she has five children to Joseph Biden's three. Five that we know about, anyway.

#28 Sarah and Todd Palin's children are christened Track, Bristol, Willow, Piper, and Trig Paxson Van Palin.

They are undoubtedly the winners of the "Worst Baby Namers in the World" Award.

HOW *NOT* TO NAME A CHILD—THE PALIN METHOD FOR BABY NAMES

Living in Alaska doesn't make you *that* removed from normal American cultural and societal norms does it, does it? Let's take a look at the most common names in America at the time the Palins' children were born:

Top Ten Names of the 1980s

Boys	Girls
Michael	Jessica
Christopher	Jennifer
Matthew	Amanda
Joshua	Ashley
David	Sarah
Daniel	Stephanie
James	Melissa
Robert	Nicole
John	Elizabeth
Joseph	Heather

Son Track was born in 1989. Rather than choose a solid Bible name for their son as the majority of Americans were doing at the time, devout Christian churchgoers Sarah and Todd chose "Track" as the unlikely moniker for their first child. The last time we looked, there was no Track in the Bible.

FAMILY FIRST (OR NOT)

Top Ten Names of the 1990s

Boys	Girls
Michael	Ashley
Christopher	Jessica
Matthew	Emily
Joshua	Sarah
Jacob	Samantha
Andrew	Brittany
Daniel	Amanda
Nicholas	Elizabeth
Tyler	Taylor
Joseph	Megan

In the 1990s, the Palins were blessed with two daughters. Rather than fall in step with the feminine christening preferences of the time, Sarah and Todd Palin chose to bestow unisex names upon their little baby girls: Bristol and Willow.

Top Ten Names of 2000

Boys	Girls
Jacob	Emily
Michael	Hannah
Matthew	Madison
Joshua	Ashley
Christopher	Sarah
Nicholas	Alexis
Andrew	Samantha
Joseph	Jessica
Daniel	Taylor
Tyler	Elizabeth

Since the turn of the century, Sarah and Todd Palin have abandoned traditional nomenclature and christened their millennial newborns with equally modern names: Piper and Trig Paxson Van.

WHERE THERE'S A WILLOW, THERE'S A WAY . . . . TO RATIONALIZE NAMING YOUR KID TRIG

Ask Sarah and Todd why they named their children the way they did, and they'll talk to you at length about it.

According to the *Washington Post*, the happy couple named their eldest child Track "after the course of the sockeye salmon the family fishes off the town of Dillingham." He was also born during the track season eighteen years ago. And Sarah's dad was supposedly a track coach. That's three good reasons for the name. (Well, at least it's three reasons.)

Daughter Bristol is named after Bristol Bay, famous for its salmon fisheries and a longtime Palin family fishing hot spot. That's two good reasons (since it's slightly less bizarre than Track, we'll buy that).

Second daughter Willow is named after the state bird, the willow ptarmigan, and a nearby town. Add the tree of the same name and you've got three (weird) reasons they chose that name.

Daughter number three, Piper, is named after the family plane. Which isn't even one good reason in our baby name book. Not that anyone asked, but it seems to us that Piper got the short end of the talking stick on this one.

But the Palins rallied when their second son was born. They outdid themselves with the name bestowed on their youngest child: Trig Paxson Van Palin. Trig is the Norse word for "brave victory." Paxson is one of Sarah's favorite spots in Alaska. And Van Palin, well, we won't spell it out for you.

Top Ten Names in Wasilla

Boys	Girls
Moose	Juneau
Hunter	Snow
Ice	Plover
Bullet	Bering
Sockeye	Honeywell
Bear	Juniper
Yukon	Sitka
Thor	Winter
R.V.	Boeing
Hawk	Raven

If the Palins are any indication, unusual names are the norm in Wasilla.

THE PALINS MAY BE ON TO SOMETHING

Studies show that unusual naming conventions are indeed becoming the norm throughout America—and not just in Alaska. In 1880, the top ten baby names were bestowed on 41 percent of boys and 23 percent of girls. But by 2006, the top ten names were bestowed on only 9.5 percent of boys and 8 percent of girls. That represents a drop of about 33 percent over the past ten years alone, according to the American Name Society. That explains why names like Mary have dropped from No. 1 back in the 1950s to No. 84 last year—and names like Nevaeh (heaven spelled backward) are making the top 100. In 2006, Nevaeh ranked No. 43 among the 1,000 most popular names in America. Go figure.

#29 Sarah Palin does not support gay marriage or spousal rights for gay couples.

... Perhaps because, like the congregants in the church she's attended since 2002, she may believe that the "power of prayer" can turn gays from homosexual to heterosexual.

Some congregations pray for peace. Some congregations pray for social justice. And some congregations, including Sarah Palin's, pray the gay away.

Palin spent most of her life as a member of the Wasilla Assembly of God, a church that's so on fire with the Holy

SARAH SAYS:

"Oh, I don't—I don't know, but I'm not one to judge and, you know, I'm from a family and from a community with many, many members of many diverse backgrounds and I'm not going to judge someone on whether they believe that homosexuality is a choice or genetic. I'm not going to judge them."

—SARAH PALIN, AS TOLD TO CHARLES GIBSON
ON *ABC NEWS*

Spirit that many members speak in tongues, though there have thus far been no reports that Palin herself has gone gonzo for glossolalia.

Since 2002, Palin has called the Wasilla Bible Church her Sunday morning home. A deeply conservative house of worship, Wasilla Bible Church espouses such potentially laudable goals as the "centrality of Christ," the "authority of scripture," and "authenticity in spiritual life" among its core beliefs.

The last one, for nonevangelicals, can be problematic. It basically translates to: "We are dogmatic in our interpretation of God's Word." Sex, except within male-female marriages (and sometimes even *that* can be suspect), is bad. Those who do not think like Wasilla Bible Church members are either thoroughly confused, misguided, or intentionally sinful.

#30 Sarah Palin's son Track is reportedly a drug addict, according to the *National Enquirer*.

Now don't scoff. The *National Enquirer* was the first to break the story on John Edwards' affair, which turned out to be true (and they're never going to let the "media elite" or any of the rest of us forget it). Well, the tabloid is at it again, trying to expose the skeletons in our Caribou Barbie's closet (and win its editors some long-awaited respect).

This time it isn't Palin's pregnant teenage daughter who's the focus, but rather her eldest son Track.

Nineteen-year-old Track, as the Republicans have been quick to point out, shipped out to Iraq September 11 amid great hoopla. But it may not be just patriotism that has motivated him to join the ranks, he might also have signed up to escape a life of drugs and crime in Wasilla, generally acknowledged to be the crystal meth capital of Alaska.

THE BAD BOY OF WASILLA

Yes, the golden son of the Palin clan is known as the "bad boy" of Wasilla, according to the *Enquirer*. Drugs—notably cocaine and Oxycontin—are his supposed favorite pastimes, allegedly along with vandalism and theft. The *Enquirer* claims that Track was a serious Oxycontin addict in 2006 and 2007, and reportedly was even main-lining the drug.

Unfortunately for Track, he partied with some very talkative people. But then, if you're all blotto on cocaine in Alaska there's nothing much to do but talk.

TRACK'S TRACK RECORD:

Here are some quotes from the *Enquirer* story from people who claim to know Track:

★ "Before joining the Army last September, Track partied all the time. I saw him do so many keg stands, and all he ever talked about was getting stoned."
★ "Track was a master at playing people and paying them to get drugs, alcohol, steal car rims, Xbox games, you name it."
★ "All the girls loved Track, but he was more into drugs and himself."
★ "I've smoked weed with Track many times. He was one of two kids in school that had a fake ID."

SARAH SAYS:

" . . . Go forth in defense of America and America's cause—and it is a righteous cause," Palin told the 4,000 troops—including son Track—at Ft. Wainright as they prepared to deploy to Iraq on September 11, 2008. "You will be there to win. . . ."

—SARAH PALIN

In Track's defense, we're talking about the *National Enquirer* here. Consider the source.

THE *NATIONAL ENQUIRER* TRUE OR FALSE GAME

The *National Enquirer* is a mix of fact and fiction. Here is a list of what they've reportedly gotten right and what they've gotten wrong. See if you can guess which ones are which.

1. Alien baby takes over New York City
2. John Edwards has love affair
3. Brad Pitt leaves Jennifer Aniston
4. Lindsay Lohan is a sloppy drunk slut
5. Grand Canyon disappears
6. Ashlee Simpson gets nose job
7. Marlon Brando rises from the dead
8. Hitler alive and living in New Jersey
9. Angelina adopts 100th child
10. Rosie O'Donnell has lesbian affair with the rest of *The View*

ANSWER KEY
1. F (That was Donald Trump)
2. T (What was he thinking—have you seen her?)
3. T (Get over it, already!)
4. T (But don't tell her mother—oops, too late for that!)
5. F (At least for now, but with global warming . . .)
6. T (Stop at one, Ashlee)
7. F (Way too fat to fly, even as a ghost)
8. F (Everyone knows he's in Brazil)
9. F (But who's counting?)
10. F (But it would be hot, though, wouldn't it?)

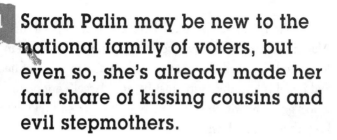

#31 **Sarah Palin may be new to the national family of voters, but even so, she's already made her fair share of kissing cousins and evil stepmothers.**

Often, you can tell a lot about someone by who likes 'em . . . and even more by who hates 'em. Sometimes, the person you want (or the person you need) gets all the right kind of people pissed off.

So who is for Sarah, and who is agin 'er?

Let's break it down . . .

DEMOCRATS

They don't like her because she's just been mayor of a tiny municipality, and has less than a full gubernatorial term in the American state that beats only Vermont, North Dakota, and Wyoming in terms of population (according to the U.S. Census Bureau). Also, she's hot, has competed in anti-feminist beauty pageants, likes to shoot guns, make moose meatloaf, and drill for oil.

RELIGIONISTS

They dig the fact that she's anti-abortion. They're not so crazy about the fact her daughter is a walking campaign for family planning, though. Christians might like the fact that Palin is a member of the Fellowship of Christian Athletes, and wore a Pat Buchanan button when that man stopped through Alaska during his abortive (oof!) Presidential campaign in '99. Jews might . . . well, Jews have no idea what to make of her, and Israel is keeping mum, just because Israel's got no idea who's going to win the election. Muslims are still trying to keep their heads down.

REPUBLICANS
The Grand Old Party loves her. They wish she would run for Queen. Think she's the best thing since Pat Boone (because not all of them know that Pat Boone is a guy).

BOOK LOVERS
They may regard her as highly suspect. According to a *National Review* article, when Palin was a mayor she asked the town librarian, three times, how the librarian would respond to a request to remove certain books from the shelves. The librarian responded that she would refuse any such request.

The mayor asked for the librarian's resignation not too long afterwards; the reasons for doing so are unclear.

ECOFREAKS
Tree huggers spaz out over the prospect of prospecting for oil in what they consider "their" territory—that is, the Alaskan wilderness. Petroleum Palin, aka Sweet Crude Sarah, has had the temerity to suggest just that very thing, thus incensing the Greenies. Heh.

RIGHT-WING POLITICAL IDEALISTS
They dig her. She went and attacked fellow Republicans
(the state attorney general and the head of the state party)
who were doing bad, bad things . . . and she was right. They
resigned, and one paid a fine.

FANS OF SMALLER GOVERNMENT
They want her to have their children. According to the *Los
Angeles Times,* she sold off the state's jet, drove her own car
while waiving off a massive security detail, and booted the
chef at the governor's mansion (because he made a miserable
moose meatloaf?).

GUN LOVERS
They are totally into her. She advocated for a state bill that
would make it easier for Alaskans to carry concealed weapons.
Cool.

BEER DRINKERS
They should want to marry her. While mayor, she fought her
own police chief when he wanted to pass a bill which would
make bars in their town close earlier.

Part 5

THE HONORABLE MAYOR
OF WASILLA

#32 Sarah Palin traces her entry into the political arena to joining the PTA in Wasilla.

Back when Sarah Palin was just "an average hockey mom," she joined the PTA in order to, as she says, "make my kids' public education better."

But, what, really, has Sarah Palin done for the "education of her kids," the oldest of whom shows little interest in higher education? (Can you even get a decent education in the state of Alaska?)

And we've seen the consequences of her support of abstinence education programs in the schools.

Let's take a closer look at her record on education.

NOW THIS IS AN EDUCATION!

1. Supports teaching creationism alongside evolution in schools. *Translation:* Dinosaurs never roamed the earth.
2. Supports charter schools. *Translation:* Alaska public schools suck.
3. Supports homeschooling. *Translation:* When you're living in the middle of nowhere, it's easier to teach at home.
4. Supports faith-based materials for homeschoolers. *Translation:* Let Go and Let God teach the little bastards.
5. Supports letting parents dismiss textbooks they find "offensive." *Translation:* Trade science book for Book of Revelations.

In fact, Palin's Alaska ranks in the bottom five states in terms of education—along with McCain's Arizona. And over the course of Governor Palin's term, Alaska's score on education has actually dropped.

ALASKANS DUMB, BUT NOT AS DUMB AS ARIZONANS

In 2006–2007, the most recent Education State Rankings, Palin's Alaska came in 46th, and McCain's Arizona came in dead last.

What does that really mean? According to Morgan Quitno Press (*www.morganquitno.com/edrank.htm*), the Smartest State Award is based on twenty-one key elementary and secondary education indicators reported from Education State Rankings, an annual reference book that compares the fifty states in hundreds of education-related categories. The award measures states based on factors including expenditures for

SARAH SAYS:

"I was just your average hockey mom, and signed up for the PTA because I wanted to make my kids' public education better."

—SARAH PALIN, AT THE
2008 REPUBLICAN NATIONAL CONVENTION

instruction; pupil-teacher ratios; high school graduation and dropout rates; and reading, writing, and math proficiency.

Vermont came in as the #1 Smartest State in the United States, with a score of 18.57.

Alaska's score: -11.91, for a rank of #46, down two ranking points from 2005–2006 (or since Sarah Palin became governor).

Arizona's score: -17.61, for a rank of #50, the same as 2005–2006.

TOP FIVE SMARTEST STATES
1. Vermont
2. Massachusetts
3. Connecticut
4. New Jersey
5. Maine

TOP FIVE STUPIDEST STATES
1. Arizona
2. Nevada
3. Mississippi
4. California
5. Alaska

According to *The Frontiersman*— Wasilla's local newspaper—Sarah Palin's response upon being questioned about her readiness for the role of mayor was that "it's not rocket science."

And yet, this is the very experience that Palin most often references when citing her qualifications to be vice president. The current mayor of Wasilla, Dianne Keller, agrees. In a statement given to the *Washington Post*, Keller states that, "Executive experience is executive experience. Whether you are a mayor or a governor or an executive at a company, the duties and responsibilities are the same."

The same? What an interesting premise. We guess that means the owner of the local Waffle House franchise is qualified to be president as well.

ROCKET SCIENCE GOVERNANCE
But for the moment, let's give both mayors—past and present—the benefit of the doubt. If correct, there's no difference in the experience necessary to govern a city of 5,500 people, whose biggest concern is how much their new hockey rink is going to cost, and overseeing a nation of more than 300,000,000 citizens whose military is immersed in a war

that—by definition—has no specific target, boundary, or means of determining victory.

Perhaps budgeting is the same as well. For example, while mayor of Wasilla, Palin's strategies took the city from having a reserve of $4 million to a long-term debt of $20 million. That's cool. Debt happens. Not a whole lot different than the national debt, which is currently sitting at a pretty $9.7 trillion, or about 485 times what Sarah's used to. Ah, it's all just numbers—hold on! That does sound a bit like rocket science! Hmm.

WHAT'S YOUR TQ?

And finally, the most important comparison: the TQ. Also known as the Telegenic Quotient. Whether you're mayor or vice president, this is the one quality above all others that qualifies you for public office. And let's face it, our Sarah knows how to work a camera. If it came down to Lincoln or Palin, you know how it would end. It's like choosing between a piece of beef jerky and filet minion. Sure, the jerky freed the slaves, but the filet looks better on TV.

POLITICS IS NO LAUGHING MATTER

"On her first day back, she shot two campaign commercials, a moose, and a caribou."

—JAY LENO

#34 In her years as a public servant, Sarah Palin has acquired a reputation as a tough boss with no qualms about firing people. Read my lipstick: You are fired!

How many people has Sarah Palin canned in her relatively brief political career? As the man once said, "The list is long, but distinguished." Here are a few highlights.

The Cop and the 'Cuda

Wasilla's founding police chief, Irl Stambaugh, came to Wasilla after a distinguished career in Anchorage law enforcement, and was the small city's founding chief of police. During a wrongful dismissal suit he brought against the 'Cuda and the city, he claimed that in her letter of termination she alleged that he had "glared sternly at her" during a number of their meetings, and she just didn't feel as if she had his support. He further stipulated that during meetings with her, he had made a point of folding his over-six-foot-over-200-pound frame into a chair and maintained both eye contact and a civil tone with her while attempting to work with her during the first few months of her administration. According to Stambaugh, another reason that the 'Cuda fired him was because several of her campaign contributors were bar owners who balked at his attempt to close down their establishments before 5:00 A.M.

The moral of the story: When the nights are as long as they are in Alaska, close the bars early at your peril.

My First Act in Office Will Be to Fire Your Ass
Palin also fired four other management-level employees in Wasilla's city government within six months of taking the job as mayor (public works director Jack Felton, finance director Duane Dvorak, library head Mary Ellen Emmons, and museum curator John Cooper). Because of the resultant public outcry, the 'Cuda eventually relented and reinstated Emmons, who at the time was president of the Alaska Library Association, and had objected when Palin explored the banning of "certain books" from the library. Emmons left Wasilla on her own, taking another job within the year.

Don't S—t Where Palin Eats
The 'Cuda was in junior high school band the first time she met John Bitney. Years later, he helped run her gubernatorial campaign. After he helped her get elected, she rewarded him by making him her legislative director, saying, "Whatever you did, you did it right," at a news conference lauding him for his outstanding work. A few weeks later, she reportedly fired him for doing a lousy job.
What really happened? According to Bitney:
John Bitney got divorced.
John Bitney started dating someone new.
That someone new was married.
Her husband called Palin.

Bitney had informed Palin that he was getting divorced, but (maybe because it wasn't any of her business?) neglected to mention the fact that he had begun dating a still-married woman. When the 'Cuda found out, Bitney later recalled, she "indicated to me that she was hurt, disappointed, and upset, and that she didn't know what she wanted to do."

So did she fire him for a personal decision unrelated to his work as her legislative director? If she did, then apparently even longtime friends aren't immune from the righteous wrath of the 'Cuda!

Job #1: Bag the Bush Moonshiners or Else!

A native of Nyac, Alaska, and a respected former Anchorage Police Chief who spearheaded a revolutionary procedural system for police to deal with the mentally ill, Walt Monegan was let go by the 'Cuda in the summer of 2008 ostensibly because he wasn't making any inroads against bush jockeys making and running (get this) "moonshine."

That's not how Monegan sees it. As reason for his termination, he points to the mound of e-mails, letters, memos, and phone calls he received from Palin, her staff, and her "First Guy" Todd, all of them reportedly calling on him to fire Palin's ex-brother-in-law, Mike Wooten, an Alaska State Trooper with a "colorful" past, and a history of short-term suspensions and reprimands.

When Monegan pointed out that Wooten's latest suspension (ten days) more than fit any malfeasance that could be proved (that pesky word) against him, First Dude Todd Palin reportedly told him Wooten "shouldn't be a trooper." Monegan explained to the Snowmobile King that "you can't head-hunt like this. What you need to do is back off, because if the trooper does make a mistake, and it is a terminable offense, it can look like political interference."

Monegan, who says of Palin herself: "She never directly asked me to fire him," has refused to make public the copies he has of his correspondence with the 'Cuda, First Oilman Todd, or any of her staff, though. He's planning to turn it all over to the retired prosecutor investigating Troopergate.

That prosecutor subpoenaed First Stud Todd Palin to testify before the committee overseeing this investigation. Wonder how Todd will remember the conversation?

And if he gets anything "wrong," will the 'Cuda fire *him*?

TOP TEN REASONS SARAH BARRACUDA MIGHT FIRE YOU

1. You looked at her funny.
2. You're too tall.
3. You married her sister.
4. You divorced her sister.
5. You're getting a divorce, and dating again.
6. You're getting a divorce, and dating a married woman.
7. You sounded "last call" at the local bar before sunrise.
8. You support the First Amendment.
9. You question the Second Amendment.
10. You were in the way.

Sarah Palin may have fired people, but she also hired people as well, leading to accusations of cronyism and favoritism.

FRIENDS AND RELATIONS

Of course, it hasn't *all* been firing. As governor, she appointed a school classmate, Franci Havemeister, to a position in the State Division of Agriculture. The job pays $95,000 a year; Havemeister, when asked about her qualifications, said that as a child she loved cows. Detractors have accused Sarah of calling those with whom she disagrees "bad people who are anti-Alaska."

SARAH STAT

The New York Times reported that Palin, "runs an administration that puts a premium on loyalty and secrecy."

TOP TEN SIGNS YOU'RE BAD
PEOPLE WHO HATE ALASKA

1. You don't like moose burgers.
2. You don't like hockey.
3. You believe in global warming.
4. You don't have the balls to shoot your own supper.
5. You don't even know where Alaska is.
6. You sure as s—t don't know where Wasilla is.
7. You take offense at the expression "Lower 48."
8. You think "Lower 48" refers to body parts.
9. You like your church and state separate.
10. You believe in dinosaurs.

Alaska is said to be the last American frontier. Unfortunately, Sarah Palin equates "frontier" with "wild west."

The *Washington Post* reports that upon taking office as mayor in October 1996, Palin immediately butted heads with then Police Chief Irl Stambaugh over "his push for moving bar closing time from 5 a.m. to 2 a.m. and for his opposition to state legislation to allow people to carry guns in banks and bars."

Well, can you blame her? Banks get robbed. Better that everyone have a gun on hand. That way when something ugly goes down, or when someone *thinks* something ugly is going down, or when someone is totally mistaken about something ugly going down, we can have multiple skittish, trigger-happy folks all pulling iron at the same time. Excellent! And we can likely do away with any security guards, because, let's face it—they'd be redundant.

And what about that push to close bars at 2 A.M. rather than 5 A.M.? Please, Mr. Police Chief, we're in Alaska. *Alaska*, for God's sake. There's nothing else to do *but* drink, so leave us to our little pleasures, would you? (It's probably not a great time to mention that, according to the Alaska Bureau of Vital Statistics, "the rate of alcohol-induced deaths in Alaska increased 16 percent between 2005 and 2006" and that "Alaska's rate has consistently remained about 2.5 times higher than the U.S. rate since 2000. The rate for Alaska Natives was over four times the rate for non-Natives.")

When considering both issues together, it appears that Palin's Christian ethics must somehow allow for drunken, late night/early morning shoot-'em-ups. Yee haw! Kill 'em all and let God sort 'em out!

TOP 5 SIGNS YOU'VE WALKED INTO A BAR IN WASILLA, ALASKA

1. The sheriff is drinking as heavily as everyone else.
2. The out-of-work security guards are working as cocktail waitresses.
3. You need an NRA membership rather than an ID to get a beer.
4. Everyone is drunk, dangerous and armed for bear— literally.
5. Happy hour ends when the sun sets, so for six months out of the year, you're gold!

POLITICS IS NO LAUGHING MATTER

"The *New York Times* had an article on problems with elderly people. They said one of the worst things that could happen to an old person is breaking a hip. The second worse thing? Losing Ohio."

—JAY LENO

37

Palin has criticized Obama for earmarks—even though her own earmark record makes for very interesting reading.

Palin has successfully convinced most of the country that she is a reformer, especially when it comes to stopping earmarks and wasteful spending. To wit: She has cut back on pork since she became governor. Yet Alaska has still asked Washington for ten times more money per citizen for specific projects than any other state. But she has consistently criticized Obama's record on earmarks . . . ?

Palin asked for a total of $198 million in earmarks this year, which is about $295 per Alaskan. Obama, on the other hand, who hasn't asked for any earmarks this year, asked for $311 million worth last year, which is about $25 for every Illinois resident. Accusing Palin of hypocrisy, Obama told Palin that ". . . words mean something; you can't just make stuff up."

MAKING HER EARMARK IN WASILLA
Before Palin became mayor, Wasilla had never sought earmarks. But Palin changed all that. In 2000, she hired an expensive lobbyist who helped Wasilla and its 7,000 residents pull in as much cash from the Congress as they could. Wasilla had joined the big leagues.

It worked. Palin and her pitbull lobbyist secured $27 million for specific projects including $15 million for a rail line from Wasilla to a ski resort. Seriously.

CALLING ALL HOCKEY MOMS

She also invested in a state-of-the-art sports complex complete with an indoor soccer field, running track, and, of course, a hockey rink—with heated seats to boot. Now that's how you go after the hockey mom vote!

In good conservative fashion, the hockey rink was built by raising taxes.

MCCAIN HAS NO APPETITE FOR PALIN PORK

According to the *L.A. Times*, McCain has called out Palin for pork barrel spending at least three times in recent years. He objected strenuously to the following earmarks requested during Palin's mayoral stint at Wasilla:

2001—$500,000 for a public transportation project in Wasilla in 2001.

2002—$1 million for an emergency communications center. (Law enforcement officials in Wasilla have called the center "redundant" and says it "creates confusion.")

2002—$450,000 for an agricultural processing facility.

PALIN EARMARKS NOT APPROVED BY CONGRESS

★ $1 million to invest in new moose stew recipes
★ $1 billion homeland security initiative to build a bridge to nowhere and then lure terrorist onto it to destroy them
★ $13 million to fund expedition to North Pole in search of Santa
★ $50 million to invest in new technology to turn snow into vanilla ice cream
★ $5 million for, well, you know, I mean, my daughter is having a baby . . . so, you know, I work hard . . .

SARAH SAYS:

"I've championed reform to end the abuses of earmark spending by Congress. In fact, I told Congress thanks, but no thanks, on that 'Bridge to Nowhere.' If our state wanted a bridge, I said, we'd build it ourselves."

—SARAH PALIN, 2008 RNC

(Read more about this Bridge to Nowhere on page 97)

THE HONORABLE MAYOR OF WASILLA

Part 6

JUST CALL ME
MISSUS GOVERNOR!

38

On September 12, 2008, the Alaska House and Senate Judiciary Committees approved thirteen subpoenas in the ongoing investigation of Governor Sarah Palin, including one for First Dude Todd Palin.

Why would saintly hockey mom Sarah be involved in such an investigation, you ask? Well, it turns out that if you mess with Sarah's sister, you mess with Sarah, too.

D*I*V*O*R*C*E

Divorces by their very nature can get u*g*l*y. A family is being "dissolved," and if kids are involved, it can be even worse.

Imagine that you're trying to divorce the sister of the governor of your state. Imagine further that you're a state employee (in this case an Alaskan state trooper).

"Okay," you think, "my sister-in-law is my boss's boss's boss," or something like that. "There's plenty of separation there. What's the worst she can do?"

If that sister-in-law is Sarah Palin, the answer is "plenty"!

Both Sarah Barracuda and her "guy" Todd reportedly wrote e-mail after e-mail to officials in this trooper's chain-of-command complaining that the trooper in question (in this case a fellow named Mike Wooten) had done everything from tasering his stepson to drinking on duty, to shooting a moose and using his wife's hunting tag for it (which is illegal in Alaska) to threatening to kill Palin's father.

Makes you wonder why the governor's *spouse* is involved in the process, doesn't it? After all, Snowmobile Racing King Todd Palin serves in no official capacity whatsoever, except to be "First Dude" to the state's chief executive.

It turns out that the trooper's union got involved, there was a hearing, and he was not terminated. The Palins reportedly responded with a flurry of e-mails venting their "disappointment" at the official finding with regard to their estranged brother-in-law.

What was the governor doing involving herself at a level so far "below her paygrade"? Good question. And why was the First Stud involved again? Better question.

The short answer is: We don't know.

SARAH SAYS:

"Concerns about Trooper Wooten's behavior were aired by both members of my family and others before Mr. Monegan ever took office as Public Safety Commissioner."

—SARAH PALIN

39

"Troopergate" bears a startlingly close resemblance to the Mother of All Gates, Watergate.

As you just read in #38, the Palins have found themselves mixed up in a bit of a scandal. You can't help but compare her situation to that of a Republican politician from years past . . .

TROOPERGATE VS. WATERGATE
Ever since G. Gordon Liddy and the gang that couldn't shoot straight got caught breaking into a Watergate Hotel–based Democratic Party office in 1972, the word "Watergate" has come to mean more than a District of Columbia hotel in American parlance. In fact, nearly every political scandal since has had the syllable "gate" appended to it as a signal to the public that someone in politics has gotten themselves into hot water again.

But the granddaddy of them all, the first one, if you will, was Watergate, and it's still the benchmark against which all American abuse-of-power scandals are measured. Not surprisingly, one of the most dishonest, disliked, and disavowed members of the political class was at the core of the Watergate scandal: its very black heart and tortured soul, if you will. For those of you in need of a scorecard, we're talking about former Republican president Richard M. Nixon.

THIS GATE'S FOR YOU
So what sort of serious Republican contender for national office would Sarah Palin be if she didn't have her own seem-

ingly petty "gate" scandal bubbling on the back burner? After all, she is a red meat (meat she presumably hunts, kills, and dresses out herself) Republican from one of the reddest of the red states; a state that has finally started putting in jail a string of lobbyists and legislators who up until last year had brazenly referred to themselves as the "corrupt bastards club." Not to worry: it turns out that Snowmobile Sarah has several scandals of her own brewing.

But we're not talking about Bristolgate (more on that in the "babies and what to do with them" section), Bridge(to Nowhere)gate (more on that in the section on non-lipsticked pork), or Planegate. Here, we're talking about Troopergate.

Troopergate bears a striking resemblance to Watergate in its potential as a cautionary tale about the possibility of abuse of executive power within a government. While Troopergate is a strictly Alaskan melodrama (at least for now) and Watergate involved the entire nation, the parallels are troubling.

COMPARING APPLES AND . . . APPLES

In both instances, the problem wasn't with the initial incident so much as with the resulting abuse of power, followed by the inevitable (non-lipsticked) ham-fisted attempts to cover up said abuse. After all, Troopergate involves something far too many of us have experienced, something often far more Machiavellian than even politics: Divorce. The Palins (both of them) have fought the Troopergate investigation (launched by the Alaska legislature) tooth and nail, citing "executive privilege" in refusing to turn over copies of the e-mails involved (just as Nixon did with the White Houses tapes). That's an asinine defense, because by including the First Dude in those communications, the 'Cuda has made a hash of any reasonable "privilege" argument.

Kinda like Nixon when he recorded his conversations.

But Miss Congeniality (yes, she really won that title, that whopper is no lie) wasn't finished yet. She turned around and fired Alaska Public Safety Commissioner Walt Monegan (her ex-bro-in-law's boss's boss's boss), reportedly because he refused to fire Mike Wooten.

Kinda like Nixon did with Attorney General Lawrence Eagleton when he refused to fire Watergate Special Prosecutor Archibald Cox.

Then she turned around and allegedly tried to get the Democratic legislator running the Alaska state legislature's investigation into whether her actions were proper dismissed. When that didn't work, she allegedly tried to get the investigation moved to a government committee that she supervises. And when that didn't work, she got a lawyer and reportedly advised all of her aides to refuse to testify before the committee investigating her conduct. As of this printing, they (and Palin's e-mails) were about to be subpoenaed.

Truly a dizzying example of near-Nixonian paranoia and arrogance, leavened with a heady dose of ugly family drama. That's Troopergate for you!

JUST CALL ME *MISSUS* GOVERNOR!

#40 Palin at first supported the now-infamous "Bridge to Nowhere," but after Congress withdrew its support, she came out against the pork barrel project—yet kept the money anyway.

When Palin was first introduced to the nation as McCain's running mate, she made sure that her fellow conservatives understood that she had a history of standing up to wasteful spending.

For those who didn't know anything about the Bridge to Nowhere, there was no reason not to believe her. But for those who did, there was nothing to do but scratch their heads (or call Charlie Gibson), and wonder how long it would be before the s—t hit the bridge. Was this woman for real?

WHERE IS THE BRIDGE TO NOWHERE?

The notorious Bridge to Nowhere, championed by Alaska Rep. Don Young, was intended to connect the small Alaskan town of Ketchikan, population 8,200, to Gravina Island, population 50 and home to the airport. The island is accessible only by ferry (and flight). Talk about a coup for the Islanders!

How much did the Alaskans ask Congress for the proposed project?

$398 million. A steal, really.

That works out to be $48,242 per person! For those of you who are math-challenged, that is: $398,000,000 divided by 8,250 (the combined populations of Ketchikan and Gravina Island) equals $48,242.

Nice pork if you can get it. And Ketchikan can!

PORK BARREL OF FUN

The earmark was so ridiculous that the project became a laughing stock in Congress—and the ultimate symbol of wasteful pork barrel spending. John McCain, an ardent critic of earmarks, was incensed. He even blamed the Republican defeat in the 2006 congressional elections on such profligate spending as the Bridge to Nowhere. In the wake of the uproar, Congress subsequently dropped the specific earmark, but allowed Alaska to keep the money to spend on transportation.

THE FLIP FLOP

The fact is, Palin did choose not to go ahead with the bridge *after* it became laughingstock, not before. What's more, she decided to keep the money Congress initially allocated for it and spend it on other things—namely, a Road to Nowhere.

We've been flipped . . . flopped.

SARAH SAYS: A SHORT HISTORY OF THE BRIDGE TO NOWHERE IN SARAH PALIN'S OWN WORDS

"Yes. I would like to see Alaska's infrastructure projects built sooner rather than later. The window is now—while our congressional delegation is in a strong position to assist."

—SARAH PALIN, *ANCHORAGE DAILY NEWS*, OCTOBER 2006

"We need to come to the defense of Southeast Alaska when proposals are on the table like the bridge, and not allow the spinmeisters to turn this project or any other into something that's so negative."

—SARAH PALIN, AUGUST 2006, *KETCHIKAN DAILY NEWS*

"I told Congress, 'Thanks, but no thanks,' on that bridge to nowhere. 'If our state wanted a bridge,' I said, 'we'd build it ourselves.'"

—SARAH PALIN, RNC, SEPTEMBER 2008

"That's the abuse that we're going to stop. That's what John McCain has promised over and over for these years and that's what I'm joining him, also, saying, you're right, the abuse of earmarks, it's un-American, it's undemocratic, and it's not going to be accepted in a McCain–Palin administration. Earmark abuse will stop."

—SARAH PALIN, AS TOLD TO CHARLIE GIBSON, *ABC NEWS*, SEPTEMBER 2008

#41 Sarah Palin's approval rating in her home state of Alaska is 80 percent—the highest of any governor in the nation.

Palin's appeal—both at home and in the nation at large—is grounded in her particularly Alaskan persona. It's a persona that might best be summed up by the local adage, "Men are men and women win the Iditarod."

The Iditarod looms large in the Alaskan imagination. Picture this: You are hanging on to an out-of-control rickshaw for dear life, in bone-chilling cold that will shatter your unprotected skin in a moment, with only a pack of howling dogs between you and death. Welcome to the Iditarod!

Virtually all Alaskans are thoroughly knowledgeable and justifiably proud of the internationally acclaimed 1,150-mile race. The Iditarod Trail Sled Dog Race runs from Anchorage to Nome across mountain ranges, frozen rivers, dense forests, desolate tundra, and windswept coastline. Riders, called "mushers," are pulled on sleds by twelve to sixteen dogs, trekking across the frozen tundra for ten to seventeen very long, very cold days. Billed as the Last Great Race on Earth, the brutally challenging competition requires a kind of stamina only the strongest can attain—and the strongest are often women. Local hero Susan Butcher won it four times.

Sarah Palin—hunter, skier, fisherwoman, marathoner, basketball star, mother of five—seems to personify the Iditarod toughness to which all Alaskans aspire. She's a tough nut to crack. Iditarod tough.

COLD RACE A HOT TOPIC FOR HOTTEST GOVERNOR OF COLDEST STATE

On September 11, 2008, vice presidential hopeful Sarah Palin returned to the state she governs to a hero's welcome. More than 1,000 supporters were there, some of them sober. The high-energy crowd was cheering as Palin and her husband descended from the plane and were greeted by her children Piper, Willow, and infant son Trig.

Palin reassured the crowd that since her announcement as John McCain's running mate, she speaks proudly of her constituents and their state wherever she goes—and always reminds her fellow Americans that Alaska is a place "where men are men and women win the Iditarod."

SARAH STAT

From the official Iditarod website: "The Iditarod Trail, now a National Historic Trail, had its beginnings as a mail and supply route from the coastal towns of Seward and Knik to the interior mining camps at Flat, Ophir, Ruby, and beyond to the west coast communities of Unalakleet, Elim, Golovin, White Mountain, and Nome. Mail and supplies went in. Gold came out. All via dog sled. Heroes were made, legends were born."

THE SECOND-TO-LAST GREAT RACE ON EARTH: THE POLITICAROD

As we have seen, Palin is all for the Iditarod. And she's all for aerial shooting of wolves and other vermin. Why not combine the two, and create a new race to the finish?

Call it the Politicarod. Pit two teams of politicians against one another, racing across the frozen tundra while the media takes potshots at them from airplanes. Whichever team crosses the barren wasteland to the Promised Land without being sniped out of commission wins four years in a much warmer—some would say boiling hot—place.

They call it the White House.

SARAH SAYS:

". . . in Alaska, like that old bumper sticker says, 'Men are men and women win the Iditarod'."

—SARAH PALIN

#42 **In 2007 Sarah Palin applied for what is believed to be her very first passport.**

ONCE UPON A TIME IN THE LAST FRONTIER . . .

For forty-three years, Palin could only imagine what life was like in other countries. Looking out at the Alaskan sky, young Palin would wonder about a world beyond Alaska. A world where children of other cultures played, prayed, and shot moose just like her.

Do they eat moose stew as well? she would ask herself. *Do they accept Jesus Christ as their personal savoir? (I do hope so—I wouldn't want them to burn in hell for all eternity!) Do they hate gays and ban books and shoot mammals for fun like me?*

Last year, Palin finally had the opportunity to find answers to her questions. After all, Palin had blossomed from that young curious child into the governor of the great state of Alaska. As part of her gubernatorial duties, she visited troops in Kuwait and Germany in 2007.

Aides say that Palin expressed concern about crossing the Atlantic Ocean, wanting to make sure that the pilots "kept their eyes on the horizon," in the unlikely but very possible event that the earth was flat.

For the trip, Palin applied for what is believed to be her first passport. She was reportedly "really excited" and asked if they could "stop by the moon" on the way to Europe.

INNOCENT ALASKANS ABROAD

We were able to locate the diary Palin kept during her trip. In this scintillating document, we found the following entries:

Germany: I am surprised how advanced the culture is here in Bratwurstland! The country has everything we have in Alaska: beer, pretzels, and crooked politicians. People are really smart, too, though they speak some kind of guttural language that I have never heard before. They also speak English, which is amazing for people who've never even set foot in Alaska. I am most impressed with the castles that seem very, very old—even older than Alaska, which God created on the very first day.

Kuwait: How strange these people are! They wear blankets on their heads in the middle of the desert, which is hot and dry because it does not get much rain. At least that is what the "scientists" say. But I think that the heat has to do with God preparing these lost Islamic souls for the eternal damnation that awaits all those who reject Christianity. Overall, I had a great trip, though. Our soldiers are really nice. I will pray for them—but not for the people of Kuwait, who will doubtless come to know their sins in the next life.

PLACES SARAH PALIN WOULD LIKE TO VISIT

PARIS: I'd like to see where Princess Diana died.

LONDON: I always wanted to see the birthplace of fish and chips.

AMSTERDAM: I hear you can get really good dope there. And it's legal and everything.

TOKYO: Sushi and saki—What more could a girl want?

MILAN: I could load up on sweaters for our tough Alaskan winters.

ROME: I was baptized Catholic as a baby, but even now that I'm a real Christian I'd like to see the Sistine Chapel. As long as I don't run into any Papists.

JERUSALEM: God told me to go to the Holy Land. He says that it's a beautiful place, except for all the Jews.

#43 Sarah Palin has been heralded for listing the private jet that once was set aside for the governor's use on eBay in an effort to sell it.

Modern legend has it that there's no better nor better-known marketplace for the buying and selling of bric-a-brac, human organs, and porn (but we repeat ourselves there) than eBay. The hoopla surrounding the story of Sarah Palin and her jet is a case in point. The only problem is, you could fly a zeppelin through the hole in that legend.

JETSETTING THINGS STRAIGHT

Unfortunately, no one on eBay took the governor up on her offer. Alaskan businessman Larry Reynolds did buy the jet, picking up the Westwind II in a private transaction for a cool $2.1 million. A good deal for Reynolds, as this amount represented a rather deep discount from Palin's eBay asking price of $2.7 million. But what's $600K between jetsetters and sellers?

JUST PLANE WRONG

John McCain waxed enthusiastically when describing his veep pick's selling skills in a Wisconsin whistle stop. "You know what I enjoy the most? She took the luxury jet that was acquired by her predecessor and sold it on eBay—and made a profit!"

Now, we don't need to get the calculator out to see that going from an asking of $2.7 million and settling for $2.1 appears to be a loss. It might be the "new math" that was busting out all over when Palin was in grade school in the '70s. Still, though, selling for less than expected doesn't usually qualify as a "profit."

JUST THE PLANE TRUTH

We know that there's nothing wrong with a political leader jetting around, especially in a place like Alaska, where much of the land is inaccessible by car. Let's be honest, Alaska is not exactly connected, geographically speaking. That's why Palin's predecessor Frank Murkowski had the jet to begin with.

I'M SARAH, FLY ME

Okay, it's undeniable that in addition to her sexy librarian look, Palin does also vaguely resemble a flight attendant, that sort of stewardess whom you know not to ask for a second packet of peanuts. But by looking at the specs of her former cherry ride, there is an opportunity to compare the two.

Westwind II	SP 2008
2,200 mile range	Several hundred–mile range (voice, unamplified)
CD stereo, wireless headsets	CDs wisely invested, constantly wired
Seating for eight	Beating for all who disagree with her
Sleek design for aerodynamic speed	Slick design for Republican greed
Two visible engines	Hidden agendas

Let's just make sure we're in upright position in the voting booths come November.

Part 7
GOD & COUNTRY

#44 The senior pastor at Palin's former church has peached that critics of President Bush would go to Hell.

The McCain camp is doing everything they can to downplay the effects of religion on Sarah Palin's world view, simply stating that she has "deep religious convictions." Yet the fact remains that she has been a practicing Pentecostal for more than twenty years, and that her church of choice until 2002, the Wasilla Assembly of God, endorses some pretty whacky views. (Palin is a current member of the Wasilla Bible Church but speaks regularly at the Wasilla Assembly of God.)

Take Ed Kalnins, the senior pastor of Wasilla Assembly of God since 1999. Kalnins has preached that critics of President Bush are going straight to hell. And here we thought we'd already been in hell for eight years.

The good pastor also doubts that St. Peter will let the people who voted for Senator John Kerry in 2004 into the pearly gates, and apparently is on the receiving end of "words of knowledge" direct from God Himself. This insider's info reveals the secret lives of strangers to him in short order—revelations that often startle the aforementioned strangers, once accosted.

PASTOR ED KALNINS ON JESUS'S "WAR MODE"

"What you see in a terrorist—that's called the invisible enemy. There has always been an invisible enemy. What you see in Iraq, basically, is a manifestation of what's going on in this unseen world called the spirit world. . . . We need to think like Jesus thinks. We are in a time and a season of war, and we need to think like that. We need to develop that instinct. We need to develop as believers the instinct that we are at war, and that war is contending for your faith. . . . Jesus called us to die. You're worried about getting hurt? He's called us to die. Listen, you know we can't even follow him unless you are willing to give up your life. . . . I believe that Jesus himself operated from that position of war mode. Everyone say 'war mode.' Now you say, wait a minute, Ed, he's like the good shepherd, he's loving all the time and he's kind all the time. Oh, yes, he is—but I also believe that he had a part of his thoughts that knew that he was in a war."

In his sermons, Pastor Kalnins often talks about the "end times" or "last days," referring to apocalyptic prophesies a certain few but highly visible Christian leaders hold dear. When Kalnins appeared with Sarah Palin at his church in June 2008, he spoke to the assembly on this theme. "I believe Alaska is one of the refuge states in the last days, and hundreds of thousands of people are going to come to the state to seek refuge and the church has to be ready to minister to them."

TOP TEN REASONS ALASKA IS A REFUGE STATE

1. There's nobody up there.
2. There's a lot of room to hide.
3. Hell, fire, and damnation don't burn in ice.
4. Satan hates snow.
5. There's enough moose for everyone.
6. Jesus packs a piece up there.
7. Hawaii is full up.
8. Eskimos are known for their hospitality.
9. There are more guns than people.
10. If you don't like it, you can escape to Canada.

SARAH SAYS:

On a $30 billion oil pipeline: "I think God's will has to be done in unifying people and companies to get that gas pipeline built. So pray for that . . . I can do my job there in developing my natural resources. But all of that doesn't do any good if the people of Alaska's heart is not good with God."

—SARAH PALIN, ADDRESSING THE WASILLA ASSEMBLY
OF GOD CHURCH IN 2008

#45 Palin attended a Pentecostal church until 2002, but is characteristically silent on the subject of her speaking in tongues.

THE SPEECH OF HER LIFE

Pundits of both parties agreed that Palin gave the best speech of the 2008 Republican convention. Still, her handlers must have heaved heaping sighs of relief that Palin didn't get up on the stump and go, "Eloha olah hay im, buh buh la oh zim bah."

What does that mean, you ask? Who knows? Who cares?

That said, meaning aside, it would have proved that the moose-stalking soccer mom was on fire with the Holy Spirit. Why? Because one of the best ways to prove that you're rolling with the Holy Ghost is glossolalia, better known to most as "speaking in tongues"—something some Pentecostals do.

FROM THE POPE TO THE PENTECOSTAL

Palin's Catholic parents joined the Wasilla Assembly of God when the future veep was only four years old. Palin remained in the Pentecostal church until 2002.

Pentecostals are basically evangelicals on steroids. Evangelicals love to shout their praise to Yahweh. But they don't believe that modern Christians have access to the same magical abilities visited upon Christ's disciples in the Book of Acts.

To wit: "Cloven tongues like as of fire" fell upon the disciples, and suddenly, "they were all filled with the Holy Ghost, and began to speak with other tongues, as the Spirit gave them utterance" (Acts 2:3–4).

Has Palin ever begun to channel the Holy Spirit and speak in some ancient language or at least in unintelligible syllables that *sound* like some ancient language? She has not, according to her former pastor Ed Kalnins.

SARAH STAT

The acclaimed documentary *Jesus Camp* details the Third Wave Movement, which trains children to fight for the Lord—with the ultimate goal being world domination. Although this "spiritual warriors" movement was renounced by the Assemblies of God in 1949, the movement is enjoying a resurgence many find troubling. The Assembly of God church that Palin attended until 2002 is reportedly part of this movement.

FAMOUS PENTECOSTALS

★ Elvis Presley
★ Jerry Lee Lewis
★ Jimmy Swaggart
★ Jim and Tammy Faye Bakker
★ James Watt
★ John Ashcroft
★ Oral Roberts
★ T.D. Jakes

SPEAK NOW . . . OR LATER

The Holy Spirit packs some powerful juju. Who knows when it might decide to manifest Itself and turn our Caribou Barbie into a nonsensical babbler? Wait a minute . . . Maybe that explains the nonsense that has poured forth from President George W. Bush for the last eight years.

On second thought . . . naah.

Sarah Palin's church supports the Love Won Out movement, designed to (among other things) turn gays straight.

"LOVE" WINS OUT IN WASILLA

What is Palin's congregation's stance on homosexuality, you ask? It is thus: Being gay is bad. Really bad. Really, really, really bad. So bad, in fact, that it must be "responded to" in a "Christ-like way" according to the August 31, 2008, Wasilla Bible Church bulletin.

Let's look at this further.

An insert in the Wasilla Bible Church bulletin reads, "You'll be encouraged by the power of God's love and His desire to transform the lives of those impacted by homosexuality."

The bulletin touts Focus on the Family's upcoming "Love Won Out" conference in Anchorage. Focus on the Family, founded by James Dobson, has received criticism for its stance on "militant feminists," intelligent design theory, gambling, and most other forms of human enjoyment. It began Love Won Out in 1998.

Gay people, so says Love Won Out, are being duped by the media (i.e., liberals) into believing such crazy notions as the theory that some people are born gay or that gay people are "normal." As a result, the ministry has taken it upon itself to show these misguided souls the error of their ways.

Through prayer and other forms of intervention, Love Won Out seeks a miracle no less challenging than when Christ turned water into wine: transforming gays into straights. This act is one of "compassion," according to Focus on the Family and to congregations such as Palin's Wasilla Bible Church.

And what of all those psychologists and psychiatrists who say this transformation isn't compassionate at all and is potentially harmful to gay people? Well, they're clearly in league with the liberal media. And all those gay people who think they don't have a problem to overcome? Forgive them, for they clearly do not have "authentic spiritual lives" as defined by Wasilla Bible Church.

So, let us join the members of Palin's congregation in prayer: "Our Father, who art in heaven, please, please, please, take the gay away. Amen."

PRAY-THE-GAY-AWAY HYMNAL

Amazing Gay-Less Grace
Jesus Loves the Little Heterosexual Children
Jesus Loves Me If I'm Straight
I Surrender All My Gay Sex Toys
In the Sweet Missionary By and By
Just As I Am . . . Not!
Old-Time Straight Religion
Turn Off This Little Light of Mine
What Gay Child Is This?

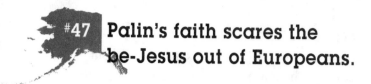

#47 Palin's faith scares the be-Jesus out of Europeans.

Europeans are overall much less religious than Americans. In fact, some 23 percent of Britons are certain there is a God, compared to some 62 percent of Americans. But the British aren't the only secularist heathens; most of the Western world isn't as gung-ho about God and Jesus as Americans. And Alaskans? Forgetaboutit.

Yes, Palin is causing quite a stir in Europe. They are fascinated with her. Some journalists like her, some don't. But most of them are a little wary of her beliefs about religion and science. Here are some excerpts from some recent articles:

IRELAND: *IRISH TIMES*
"Who literally believes that Jonah made his home in a whale's abdomen? Nobody really, apart from the U.S. president—and the woman who was recently added to the 2008 Republican ticket. . . . Sarah Palin is the latest politician to carry the torch of science misinformation tainted by religious dogma lit during the Reagan administration and nurtured by George Bush. . . . Yet centuries after the Enlightenment, Sarah Palin, the putative U.S. vice-president, can endorse the passing off of Bible stories as scientific facts, dressed up as the oxymoronic term 'creationist science.'"

GERMANY: *DER SPIEGEL*

"Sarah Palin's Pentacostalist [sic] past explains a lot about what she says in public, but the McCain campaign wants to play it down. Can a gas pipeline really be a manifestation of God's will? . . . Sarah Palin has shown a habit of investing secular matters with religious meaning. . . . Palin acts as though all political decisions emanated directly from a divine resolution—and as if the Republican understanding of this resolution were the only one that could be correct."

SPAIN: *EL PAÍS*

Palin is: "a figure who comes from the America that is far-thest removed from, and incomprehensible to, the European spectator . . . [who] represents values and policy proposals . . . the outlawing of abortion, the preponderance of religious faith, the supremacy of the traditional family, the subjection of the State to individual initiative. . . ."

POLITICS IS NO LAUGHING MATTER

"Sarah Palin has been getting briefed on what she needs to know to be John McCain's vice president. The first thing they taught her was CPR.

—CONAN O'BRIEN

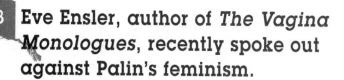

#48 Eve Ensler, author of *The Vagina Monologues*, recently spoke out against Palin's feminism.

The feminist force has come out to put an end to any hopes the former beauty queen has of taking the VP title. A leading voice in this battle against political Barbie is *Vagina Monologues* author, Eve Ensler. Ensler unleashed a scathing anti-Palin tirade on why the woman McCain tapped to be his number-two would do crap for feminism.

Ensler wrote, "[E]very thing Sarah Palin believes in and practices is antithetical to feminism, which for me is part of one story—connected to saving the earth, ending racism, empowering women, giving young girls options, opening our minds, deepening tolerance, and ending violence and war."

On top of the fact that Palin doesn't believe in evolution or abortion, Ensler argues she's against free thinking as well. How could a *woman* not support independent thought, another woman's right to choose, or the idea that females didn't spring from the rib of a man? It makes you question what Palin's own vagina is thinking . . .

THE SARAH PALIN VAGINA MONOLOGUE

I never thought of my vagina as being independent, or capable of free thought, or even gave it a chance to question and breathe between pregnancies. But if I did, I wonder what it would say? Would it be happy with me? Is it cold up here in

*Alaska? I'm sure it'd prefer the warm springs of DC and see-
ing the cherry blossoms budding and popping—and speaking
of popping cherries, how does it feel about being a grandmother? Does it appreciate the fact that one of the babies it
bore now has her own?*

*I feel like I need to be in better touch with my vagina. I
never thought to ask it how it would feel about being the first
vice presidential vagina ever. And I'm sure no one thought
of it when my name was first tossed around. No one asked it
how qualified I am during the vetting process. No one both-
ered to check its track record, or see how it feels with being
thrust into the spotlight.*

*But now that it is in the spotlight, I need to care for it.
People always criticize Hillary Clinton for abandoning her
vagina while playing the political game. I don't want my
vagina to feel abandoned. My vagina is not Hillary Clinton's
vagina. It is a political vagina on to itself.*

*I've never thought about the political power my vagina
possesses. It's always been so busy giving birth, training for
marathons, and playing hockey mom vagina that I've never
let it think about the role it plays as governor vagina and
would assume as vice president vagina. I need to embrace my
political vagina.*

*My vagina is a powerful vagina. I love my powerful
vagina.*

VAGINAS ASIDE

You have to wonder what this potential VP would do with the power given to her with a Republican win. Palin is reputed to be pro–book banning and seen as antifeminist. So what would happen with a combination of the two times vice presidential power? One could only imagine, but our advice is to buy a copy of each of the following before they become permanently out of stock:

SHORTLIST FOR THE BANNED BY PALIN PRIZE

★ *The Feminine Mystique* by Betty Friedan
★ *The Vagina Monologues* by Eve Ensler
★ *The Color Purple* by Alice Walker
★ *Herland* by Charlotte Perkins Gilman
★ *Their Eyes Were Watching God* by Zora Neale Hurston
★ *The Second Sex* by Simone De Beauvoir
★ *101 Things You—and John McCain—Didn't Know about Sarah Palin* by Gregory Bergman

49

Sarah Palin does not support explicit sex-ed programs in Alaska.

However, the plucky Palin conveniently forgets that raging hormones and abstinence do not mix. And now, as the real-life revival of the 2007 cinematic hit *Juno* plays out in Juneau—in the Palin household, no less!—we are reminded that teens like to have sex. Namely, seventeen-year-old Bristol Palin and her beau, Levi Johnston. On Labor Day (how appropriate!), the Palin camp announced that daughter Bristol is five months pregnant, and the governor and the First Dude issued a statement saying they are "proud of Bristol's decision to have her baby and even prouder to become grandparents."

JUNO IN JUNEAU

Like Ellen Page's eponymous character in the movie *Juno*, Bristol is with child, and reportedly having the child. Levi, the real-life daddy is nothing like Michael Cera's character, who in the movie has sex once with Juno and runs everywhere in a goofy track outfit. Based on Facebook pics, Levi dresses like a redneck and is more into shooting stuff than running, but Sarah likes running, so that's close enough.

In the movie, Jennifer Garner's character is married to Jason Bateman's character and they plan on adopting Juno's baby, which is funny because at the time of publication, Jennifer Garner is pregnant in real life with Ben Affleck's baby and he's best friends with Matt Damon, who seems to hate Sarah

Palin, who just happens to be supporting Bristol just like Juno's parents did in the movie. But the plot thickens as Grandma is a VP contender and suddenly fact feels more interesting than fiction. But we digress.

There's no chance of a spoiler in this movie review, since Bristol isn't due until December. Invite-only early releases slated for Wasilla, Anchorage, and possibly Washington, D.C.

SARAH STAT

$1.5 billion has been spent on abstinence-only programs in the last ten years. During the same period, birthrates for teens rose for the first time in fifteen years, according to the National Center for Health Statistics. Guess those kids just said no to abstinence.

SARAH SAYS:

"I like running the hills, it kills me. That's why I like it; I mean, it thrashes your guts and your lungs and your thighs . . ."

—A SVELTE SARAH PALIN, AFTER AN URBAN HIKE
WITH BLOGGER SCOTT SLONE IN ABOUT HER SEVENTH
MONTH OF PREGNANCY

50

Sarah Palin is a member of the NRA and an avid hunter, two qualifiers often associated with the GOP.

Palin's support of the Second Amendment is also well-known and documented. Because of her affinity for guns and hunting, some have compared Palin to past Republican hunters, including one of our nation's most famous presidents, Teddy Roosevelt. Whether or not those photos of Palin gutting a moose will surface is questionable, and seeing pictures of Roosevelt in front of a dead rhinoceros may be difficult to stomach. At a quick glance, one could see some truths in a comparison of the Rough Rider to the Hockey Mom.

But don't let that deceive you. Sure, Teddy's Oyster Bay Victorian may have a buffalo head over the fireplace in the entryway, a polar bear skin rug in his wife's parlor, and an elephant foot trashcan in his great receiving room. And what Alaskan girl *hasn't* enjoyed the thrill of hunting the first buck of the season? Teddy may have gone on countless safaris and hunting trips, but he wasn't all bad. Before you call PETA to help sponsor the removal of Roosevelt's face from Mt. Rushmore, consider the following facts.

TEDDY THE TREE HUGGER
T.R. was a pioneer in the conservation movement, and modern-day tree huggers that would otherwise condemn him for his

hunting should thank the trust-buster. Besides his role as a hunter, Roosevelt was also a naturalist, and he preserved 230 million acres of wildlife habitat across the United States. Today, this vast amount of land makes up some of our national forests, national parks, and wildlife refuges. In sum, Roosevelt created 150 national forests, 51 federal bird reservations, 18 national monuments, 5 national parks, and 4 national game preserves.

DO WE *REALLY* NEED ALL THAT WILDLIFE PROTECTION?

In August 2008, news reports detailed Sarah Palin's support of increased oil and gas drilling in environmentally sensitive areas. She supports a controversial predator control program that allows for the aerial shooting of wolves and bears. She opposed federal action to list the polar bear as a species threatened by extinction, and opposes protections for beluga whales found in the Cook Inlet, a potential site for oil and gas drilling. Palin supports construction of one of biggest mining complexes in the world at Bristol Bay, site of the world's largest sockeye salmon fishery. Finally, the Arctic National Wildlife Refuge is a favored drilling place for Palin.

SHE'S NO TEDDY ROOSEVELT

Yes, Palin and Roosevelt share a love of hunting. But while Roosevelt was ahead of his time realizing that conservation was necessary to protect his favorite pastime, Palin's environmental policies could set us back 100 years or more. Right back to around the time Teddy was vice president.

Now that's what we call progress.

#51 Sarah Palin is as full of contradictions as her beloved home state of Alaska.

Alaska is a state of contradictions. It is at once fiercely independent (the Alaskan Independence Party wants to secede from the union), and desperately reliant on the federal government (Alaska receives more earmarks per capita than any other state). It is at once the biggest state in the union (roughly twice the area of Texas) and the smallest (the population is approximately 670,000). It is at once a place where the sun doesn't shine for half the year, and a place where it won't *stop* shinning for the other half.

It is only this strange and intriguing state that could nurture a character like our Caribou Barbie. Like Alaska, Palin is a walking contradiction:

★ She prides herself on being a fiscal conservative. / She left Wasilla with its first deficit during her tenure.
★ She believes in abstinence-only education. / Her daughter is a pregnant teenager.
★ She runs on a platform of "reform." / She is currently under investigation for unethical conduct.
★ She is a beauty pageant winner. / She kills, and skins, and eats wild game.
★ She has great friends / Her friends won't automatically vote for her.

- ★ She's married to hot First Dude. / She allegedly screwed around with his partner.
- ★ She loves high heels. / She can't wear them hunting.
- ★ She went to five colleges. / Her kids have shown little interest in attending even one college.
- ★ She loves America. / She wants to run it into the ground.

ALASKA FACTS

Here's more than you ever wanted to know about Palin's home state—but it explains a lot. Alaska is a beautiful, brutal country all its own. It's all-American and completely alien at the same time. Here's proof.

DID YOU KNOW?

Fossil: Woolly mammoth

Flower: Forget-me-not

Mammal: Moose

Fish: King salmon

Bird: Ptarmigan

Insect: Dragonfly

Tree: Sitka spruce

Sport: Dog mushing

Mineral: Gold

Gem: Jade

MORE DID YOU KNOW?

1. Alaska was first discovered in 1741 by Danish explorer Vitus Jonassen Bering on a voyage from Siberia.
2. The first settlement was established in Alaska in 1784 by Russian whalers and fur traders on Kodiak Island.
3. U.S. Secretary of State William H. Seward bought Alaska from Russia for $7,200,000, or two cents per acre in 1867.

4. On October 18, 1867, Alaska officially became the property of the United States. Many Americans called the purchase "Seward's Folly."

5. The gold rush era started in 1880 with Joe Juneau's discovery of the precious metal.

6. The first battle fought in America since the Civil War occurred in Alaska when Japan invaded the Aleutian Islands, starting the One Thousand-Mile War in 1943.

7. Alaska officially became the 49th state on January 3, 1959.

8. Alaska produces 25 percent of the United States' oil.

9. "Alaska native" refers to the original inhabitants of Alaska—including Aleut, Eskimo, and Indian groups.

10. The only parts of North America occupied by Japanese troops during World War II were Agattu, Attu, and Kiska.

11. Alaska's Mt. McKinley is the highest point in North America at 20,320 feet above sea level.

12. The record high temperature in Alaska was 100 degrees Fahrenheit at Fort Yukon in 1915; the record low temperature was –80 degrees Fahrenheit at Prospect Creek Camp in 1971.

Learn more facts about ALL the states at: www.50states.com/facts/alaska.htm

#52 Early in 2008, Palin cut funding for a state program benefiting teen mothers that provided guidance, support, and shelter.

So you thought a woman personally connected to an instance of teen pregnancy would be more open to supporting teen moms in Alaska? Think again. Don't go underestimating our Caribou Barbie.

HOME SWEET HOME—NOT!

The program, Covenant House Alaska, is a combination of shelters and programs for youths in trouble and in need. Covenant House also supports funding for Passage House, a transitional living program for teen mothers. Passage House provides a safe and supporting environment for these young mothers and their babies to live for up to eighteen months while they gain essential skills and resources to make better lives for themselves and their newborns.

In April 2008, Palin went through a spending bill passed by the Alaskan legislature and reduced funding for (or eliminated completely) the programs she opposed. According to the *Washington Post*, Palin cut funding for Covenant House Alaska from $5 million to $3.9 million, or more than 20 percent.

As a mother of five, Palin knows the support systems mothers need to raise a child, whether emotional, mental, or financial. Palin's own daughter, Bristol, was announced as five months pregnant in September 2008, sparking more controversy around Palin and her family. We're sure that Palin will share her mothering know-how with Bristol—but here's some of it for other unwed pregnant teenagers.

TOP TEN SURVIVAL TIPS FOR TEEN MOMS
1. Move into the governor's mansion.
2. Use field-dressing rags for diapers.
3. Find a GILF to babysit.
4. Have Daddy First Dude arrange a shotgun wedding.
5. Have Daddy first Dude arrange a hunting accident.
6. Learn to make a mean moose stew.
7. Trade in your regular hunting togs for bib waders.
8. Milk your own caribou milk.
9. Have your mom pretend the baby is hers.
10. Give your baby up for adoption to a nice Eskimo family.

POLITICS IS NO LAUGHING MATTER
"An activist in Alaska is trying to get Sarah Palin to release 1,000 e-mails that she is withholding from the public. Apparently some e-mails went unanswered with the subject line, 'Mom I Need to Talk With You About Birth Control.'"

—CONAN O'BRIEN

GOD & COUNTRY

Part 8
POLICIES & PLANS

#53 Sarah Palin's support of expanding oil operations is greeted by supporters cheering, "Drill, baby, drill"!

When it comes to energy and finding new sources of oil in the United States, our gal Palin believes in drilling down to essentials. While some of the rest of us might be worried about destroying parts of Alaska through massive exploitation, she thinks there's no problem at all—although the moose and caribou might disagree.

SARAH WOOS JOHN'S SWITCH

McCain himself was until recently opposed to drilling in the Alaskan National Wildlife Refuge. Sensing a chance to pander to the right wing of the party, he flipped his position and came out *for* drilling. So it must have been comforting for him to realize his running mate is positively ecstatic on the subject. If McCain is for drilling, she's for drilling absolutely. If he feels little concern about the fate of the wildlife in the area, she's certain drilling for oil would be good for the beavers in the area.

Attendees of the Republican National Convention evidently agreed, chanting "Drill, baby, drill!" during Sarah's speech.

Of course, as has been pointed out numerous times, since oil is traded on the world market, which sets the price, even if we found oil in Alaska tomorrow, it wouldn't have a significant impact on world prices and hence on our pain at the pump. In fact, most experts predict it would be at least ten years before oil found in Alaska would have any impact at all on prices.

Still, reality has never been a tax-paying citizen in Sarah's La La Land.

SARAH SAYS:

"I think those politicians who don't understand that we need more domestic supply of energy flowing into our hungry markets, you know, they're living in La-La Land. And we're in a world of hurt if their agenda continues to be to lock up these safe, secure domestic supplies of energy."

—SARAH PALIN, SPEAKING ON CNBC'S
KUDLOW & COMPANY IN JUNE 2008

Roast Beaver
with Sauerkraut

Serves
3-4

Serve this dish with extra mustard and thick slices of rye or pumpernickel bread and butter. Don't forget the beer.

1 small beaver, dressed out and whole

1 (28-ounce) jar or can of sauerkraut

1 beer, light or dark

2 tablespoons or more German-style grainy mustard

Kosher salt and freshly ground black pepper to taste

1. Place beaver in pot of salted water and bring to a boil. Lower heat and simmer for 1 hour, until slightly tender. Remove from pot and while warm, scrape off all the fat. Empty the water from the pot.
2. Place beaver back in the pot and add sauerkraut, beer, mustard, and salt and pepper to taste. Simmer for about an hour or until meat falls from the bones. Serve in shallow bowls.

Sarah's Cooking Tip

If you're not lucky enough to live in Beaver Land, you can substitute opossum in this recipe.

#54 Palin has sued the federal government for putting polar bears on the endangered species list.

Polar bears may be the largest predators on land, but they've got nothing on Caribou Barbie. The 1,500-pound mammals have met their match in Sarah Palin. Palin might normally want to keep these formidable beasts around—imagine one of these babies stuffed!—but the noble creatures have committed the one sin Caribou Barbie cannot tolerate. They are in the way—of future oil and gas developments, that is.

Palin wants to drill for oil on the state's northern and northwestern coasts, the prime habitat of polar bears in Alaska. But she can't do that if the polar bear is listed on the endangered species list.

ENTER THE GRIZZLY LAWYERS

Palin contends that the bears are just fine—not endangered at all. In fact, she says that the number of polar bears has "risen dramatically over the last thirty years." Of course, that isn't true. (The population went up in the 1970s briefly because of more aggressive antihunting measures taken by the state.) Since then, however, polar bear populations are declining because the ice caps in their habitat are melting, which scientists attribute to global warming. The polar bear is the first animal to gain such protection because of climate change, but probably not the last.

A U.S. Geological Survey study completed in 2007 predicted polar bears in Alaska could be wiped out by 2050.

But who's counting?

POLAR BEARS: A BRIEF STUDY

The polar bear (*Ursus maritimus*) is native to the Arctic and its surrounding areas. It's the world's largest predator found on land, with an adult male weighing around 880–1,500 pounds and an adult female being about half that size. These creatures have many characteristics adapted for cold temperatures. They are able to move across snow, ice, and open water. Although born on land, polar bears spend much of their time on the ice, hunting seals.

Polar bears are in danger. The species is classified as a vulnerable species. There are nineteen recognized polar bear subpopulations. Five are declining, five are stable, two are increasing, and seven have insufficient data. The polar bear is a key symbol in the cultural life of Arctic indigenous peoples. It has been and continues to be important to them both as a spiritual figure and material source.

WHY PALIN HATES POLAR BEARS

★ They are not as cuddly up close as they are in cartoons.
★ They don't understand the importance of energy independence.
★ Too gamey for a good stew—but try a roast (see recipe that follows)!
★ They wear white after Labor Day.
★ They are probably not even Christians.

Brisket-Style
Bear Roast

Serves
10–12

The cooking time of a bear roast or other wild game fluctuates greatly depending on the age of the animal. Younger animals will be more tender and will cook more quickly. Older animals need more liquid for brining or braising and may require marinating for 1 or 2 days, refrigerated.

1 (5- to 6-pound) bear roast

¼ cup grainy German-style mustard

Coarse kosher salt and freshly cracked pepper to taste

2 cups beef bouillon

1 cup red wine

2 tablespoons soy sauce

Zest and juice of 1 lemon

4 cloves garlic, minced

1 tablespoon gingerroot, shredded

Precaution

Take caution in cooking bear; it is known to carry the parasite that causes the illness trichinosis. Freezing does not kill the parasite. Cooking bear meat to an internal temperature of at least 140°F is the safest way to ensure that the parasite is killed. Many prefer bear cooked well-done for safety's sake.

1. Preheat oven to 275°F.
2. Place roast in a large pan. Spread with mustard and sprinkle with salt and pepper.
3. Combine beef bouillon, red wine, soy sauce, lemon zest and juice, garlic, and gingerroot. Pour over roast. Place in the oven and bake, uncovered. Baste with sauce every 20 to 30 minutes until well glazed. After 3 hours, cover tightly with heavy-duty foil and bake for an additional 2 to 3 hours or until meat is well-done and fork tender.

EVOLVE, POLAR BEARS, EVOLVE!

Even if the polar bears *are* in trouble, so what? Okay, so they may have to swim a little more from iceberg to iceberg because the ice caps are melting, but that's just going to make the toughest and strongest bears persevere. And after all, our Caribou Barbie probably reasons that if those so-called "scientists" at the EPA really believe in evolution, then why don't the polar bears just evolve already and learn to swim better. Palin's got some drilling to do.

Drill, baby, drill!

SARAH SAYS:

" . . . we are suing the federal government, recognizing that the Endangered Species Act is not a place to kind of mess around with in terms of listing as threatened a species that right now is very, very healthy. In fact, the number of polar bear has risen dramatically in the last thirty years. Our fear being that extreme environmentalists will use this tool, the ESA, to eventually just curtail or halt North Slope production of very rich resources that America needs."

—SARAH PALIN

#55 When it comes to exploiting natural resources, Palin seems to be a little . . . oily.

Governor Palin's stance on drilling for natural resources is an odd mix of "maverick" tactics and "oilman" devotion to special interests. It must make John McCain's head spin.

As a maverick, Governor Palin passed substantial tax increases on state oil production. To be sure, this move pissed off plenty of oil companies. Hooray! And yet, consider the following:

During a recent speech in Nevada, Palin stated that she would firmly back the Republican doctrine calling for increased drilling for offshore oil. This statement led to the now famous retort from the crowd of "drill, baby, drill!" The cheer has since caught on and can be seen adorning souvenir T-shirts sold at brothels throughout the state.

And a recent *New York Times* article reports that Palin believes Alaska's economic future is tied to "aggressively extracting its vast natural resources." Ah, that's the spirit. Thinking like a hunter. Track it, shoot it, bring it home to Pa.

SALMONIZE IT!

And while she purports to being a defender of the environment, within days of making the comment above, she opposed a ballot designed to aid in the protection of salmon from mining contaminants.

Additionally, Palin's chief advisor on Alaska's proposed natural gas pipeline is a former lobbyist for TransCanada, the very firm to whom Palin is giving a $500 million subsidy to build the project in the first place.

FIRST DUDE DOES OIL

And finally, consider Palin's husband, Todd. Todd works for BP (that's right: "Big-Ass Petroleum"). And he's not just

SARAH SAYS:

"Our opponents say, again and again, that drilling will not solve all of America's energy problems—as if we all didn't know that already. But the fact that drilling won't solve every problem is no excuse to do nothing at all. Starting in January, in a McCain-Palin administration, we're going to lay more pipelines . . . build more new-clear[sic] plants . . . create jobs with clean coal . . . and move forward on solar, wind, geothermal, and other alternative sources."

—SARAH PALIN, AT THE
2008 REPUBLICAN NATIONAL CONVENTION

pumping gas and checking the air in your tires. So it wouldn't be a stretch to assume that Palin's efforts are all about making sure her husband has something to do during the day (conflict of interests be damned!).

CATCH 22

Adding a slight complication to the matter is the fact that Todd also owns his own fishing business. Think about it—the poor bastard is getting screwed no matter how things turn out. Either he's limited on how much he can drill, but his fish thrive, or he can drill to his heart's content, but his fish all get cancer and die. Some days a guy just can't win!

#56 Sarah Palin defines herself as a fiscal conservative, but the veracity of that statement depends upon how you define *fiscal conservative*.

In the lexicon of modern American political conservatism, few words are given as much weight as these two: "fiscal conservatism." Seriously, they rank right up there with "pro-life," "N.R.A.," and "nucular"!

And, of course, ever since she got the veep nod from St. John the Reformer, Sarah Palin has been flashing her bonafides as a "fiscal conservative" in speech after speech. Insert here the ludicrous assertion that she somehow said "thanks, but no thanks" to the Feds when they tried to force her to take the 300-plus million bucks that would pay for that much-needed "Bridge to Nowhere" before it actually became a punchline on late-night talk shows.

So Sarah Palin is a "fiscal conservative"? Really? Since when?

THE FISCALLY CONSERVATIVE MAYOR
OF WASILLA

Since she was mayor of Wasilla, Alaska? If Palin was such a "fiscal conservative" during her tenure as mayor of Wasilla, then why did she raise the sales tax (even on food) to a crushing rate while mayor of Wasilla? While it's true that she cut corporate taxes to the bone, people in Wasilla saw their individual tax rates skyrocket during her time in office. That's what we call robbing Peter to pay Paul.

That also begs the question: if she's so fiscally responsible, why did she leave office as mayor of Wasilla with the city burdened by a $6 million debt? What was the municipal debt level when she took office during the late 1990s, you ask? ZERO.

SARAH SAYS:

"That's what John McCain has promised over and over for these years and that's what I'm joining him, also, saying, you're right, the abuse of earmarks, it's un-American, it's undemocratic, and it's not going to be accepted in a McCain-Palin administration. Earmark abuse will stop."

—SARAH PALIN

THE FISCALLY CONSERVATIVE GOVERNOR
OF ALASKA

Okay, so maybe she wasn't a fiscal conservative while she was mayor. Maybe the 'Cuda had a change of heart afterward, and has operated as one since getting elected governor in 2006?

If that's the case, then why is she insisting on borrowing money for the state to pay for necessities such as road maintenance (those roads she can't get the Feds to pay for, that is) while the state is enjoying record surpluses in revenue because of high oil prices? The short answer: It's a lot more fun to give that money away directly to voters, oops, we mean taxpayers.

POLITICS IS NO LAUGHING MATTER

"Sarah Palin took a break. She went back to Alaska. Now people can go back to ignoring John McCain."

—JAY LENO

#57 Cindy McCain is redefining national security experience—in Sarah Palin's favor.

In a bold move, Cindy McCain proclaimed Sarah McCain an expert in national security due to Alaska's proximity to Russia. The second wife of John McCain actually said that Sarah Palin had a "unique perspective" on national security because Russia is right next door to Alaska.

"You know, the experience that she comes from is," Cindy McCain told ABC, "what she has done in government—and remember that Alaska is the closest part of our continent to Russia."

Really? Then the Eskimos have a lot of foreign policy experience too, considering that their ancestors crossed the Bering Strait from the Russian continent to the North American continent some 10,000 years ago. Must be in their blood.

Steve Doocy of *Fox News* has made similar statements. Since when does distance become the determining factor on a policy adviser's resume?

Given this rationale, Palin's national security experience is looking better and better.

ALASKA: YOU ARE HERE

Check out the mileage, and you'll see that Palin must be an expert on all these countries. (I guess the governors of California, New Mexico, and Texas are experienced in national security policy as well. And what about the states bordering Canada? No wait, never mind, that's just silly.)

ANCHORAGE TO:

Moscow: 4,635 miles   *Beijing:* 4,001 miles
London: 4,481 miles   *Baghdad:* 5,883 miles
Tokyo: 3,487 miles   *Sydney:* 7,350 miles
Paris: 4,687 miles   *Washington, D.C.:* 3,346 miles

WORLD WAR III SOUNDS FINE TO ME

Palin asserts that Georgia and Ukraine should be admitted to NATO, and that the United States should be prepared to go to war if Russia invades Georgia again. Good idea. Looks like Palin really is a pitbill—she certainly has the IQ of one.

THE PALIN DOCTRINE

Given her murky understanding of the Bush Doctrine (see page 172), Palin is working on her own foreign policy doctrine. It is basically a mishmash of tough-sounding rhetoric and occasional conversations with God—kind of like the Bush Doctrine. So it's hard to understand what she doesn't understand about the Bush Doctrine.

Palin has also linked the war in Iraq to the terrorist attacks on 9/11, a view even Bush now rejects.

SARAH STAT

She has never once met with a foreign head of state. But given her proximity to them all, we're sure they'll be dropping by Wasilla for a little moose stew any minute now.

#58 When questioned about her knowledge of foreign affairs, Palin notes that her experience with Russia is unique. So unique, in fact, that only Eskimos and polar bears can claim a closer relationship.

Palin's supporters note that Alaska's "proximity" to Russia has given her unique experience on foreign affairs. No less than Cindy McCain states that, "Remember that Alaska is the closest part of our continent to Russia." (See page 143 for more.) Thanks for clearing that up, Cindy. Now go back to your sorority house and spend some "quality time" with the BMOC.

Apparently being able to "see" Russia from an island off the coast is the same as actually working with the Russians. Let's follow this line of logic a tad further, shall we?

★ Massachusetts is the closest state to Algeria so, undoubtedly, Governor Deval Patrick should be claiming that as his basis for foreign affairs experience.

★ Hawaii is just a hop, skip, and a jump from China, so *clearly* Governor Linda Lingle is our go-to person for all things Chinese. How could she not be?

★ Nepalese Sherpa are up really high in the mountains, so on that fateful day when Mars finally attacks, we know who to go to for leadership.

TOP TEN THINGS THAT QUALIFY YOU TO DO OTHER THINGS

1. Eating an entire bag of donut holes qualifies you to be a pastry chef.
2. Owning a fish bowl gives you the cred to host a documentary on sea life.
3. Making a paper airplane means that you, too, can be a "top gun."
4. Watching the *Bourne* films qualifies you to be a spy—or an actor.
5. Wearing a white disco suit ensures you've got everything you need to "stay alive."
6. Looking really hard at the sun makes you an astronomer (and blind).
7. Breaking the speed limit suggests a career in Nascar or a role opposite Jackie Gleason's corpse in a *Smokey and the Bandit* remake.
8. Wearing glasses makes you an optometrist. Or perhaps Tina Fey.
9. Smoking pot qualifies you for the DEA, or possibly as a dealer for Sarah Palin. Sure, she didn't like it. I guess the "I didn't inhale" excuse was already taken.
10. Taking a crap makes you a plumber.

Part 9

HOBBIES & SPECIAL
INTEREST (GROUPS)

#59 **Sarah Palin continues the gun-toting standard set by the most famous vice president with a gun—current VP Dick Cheney.**

The question (the one we're most interested in) is: Which of these hard-as-fake-nails veeps would win in a showdown?

According to a recent *Newsweek* article online, Palin has either been a longtime member of the NRA, or a lifetime member of the NRA (there is a difference, especially to armed chicks). Palin loves to hunt, and has a penchant for moose stew (see page 221). *Moose. Stew.* Let's think about that for a second: According to the State of Alaska's Department of Fish and Wildlife, moose are some damned big animals. Adult moose run from 800 all the way up to 1,600 pounds! Now, let's compare that to your average trial attorney. According to the CDC, average American adults weigh between about 164 and 191 pounds. So, for every time Palin takes down even a scrawny moose, Cheney needs to cap a minimum of four big-ass lawyers. In the face.

Whom would you rather arm to support you during the zombie invasion? We don't think there's much question. But just in case you remain unconvinced:

Bullet by Bullet Comparison of Sarah and Dick

Sarah Palin	Dick Cheney
Fired on the good old boys in Anchorage	Fired on his hunting buddy.
Eats moose for breakfast	Eats heart-healthy Quaker Oats for breakfast
Wears killer pumps	Dresses like, well, a Republican

SARAH SAYS:

"I do not, and, you know, here again, life being an open book here, as a candidate, I'm a lifetime member of the NRA. I believe strongly in our Second Amendment rights. That's kind of inherent in the people of my state who rely on guns for not just self-protection, but also for our hunting and for sports, also. It's a part of a culture here in Alaska. I've just grown up with that."

—SARAH PALIN, AS TOLD TO
CHARLIE GIBSON ON *ABC NEWS*

#60   One impressive, even intimidating, skill Sarah Palin brings to the table is her ability to field dress any large mammal she takes down.

Who needs foreign policy experience or the ability to define the Bush Doctrine when you can eviscerate a moose?

Certainly not Sarah Palin. The Palinator may not know how to spell Putin, even though you can, like, totally *see* Russia from parts of Alaska, as she has excitedly pointed out. But many conservatives are willing to overlook her shortcomings because Palin is able to hunt, kill, and field dress the state animal of the Land of the Midnight Sun. In fact, she's so tough that she probably harbors fantasies of field dressing more than wild game. Imagine what might happen if Palin were to get fed up with her new life under the microscope. Her father, with his large collection of stuffed wildlife, might have his hands full stocking display cases with his daughter's new quarry.

★ Palin would probably start with Hillary Clinton. In addition to being a flaming liberal, Hillary's a loser and the person Palin is intended to supplant for the white female vote. Palin would bring her down and mount her in one of Hillary's annoying pantsuits.

★ Rather than gutting Bill Clinton, Palin would probably just chop up Bill's marriage vow–denying bad-boy bits and use them for fish bait.

★ Barack Obama. Joe Biden. Nancy Pelosi. 'Nuff said.

* Once Palin gets a taste for blood, she'll turn to liberal mouthpieces. She would probably just feed most of the news and editorial staff of the *New York Times* to her woodchipper (surely she has one), saving only managing editor, Jill Abramson, as a trophy.
* Since she'll already be in New York, Palin then can turn to the talking heads associated with famously liberal MSNBC. Just imagine Palin giggling girlishly as she debones Keith Olbermann during one of his endless special comments.
* Palin may decide to drop in on *Saturday Night Live*'s Tina Fey and field dress her for doing such a dead-on impression of the Alaskan governor.
* By this time, there will be no stopping the Palinator. She'll pay a visit to rotund liberal blowhard Michael Moore and to uberliberal chanteuse Barbra Streisand. Just Streisand's famous nose alone would be a feast for Alaska's schools of rockfish, whitefish, and longnose suckers.
* Palin might even make a swing through the South and try to find the B-52s, whose female members had the temerity to adopt Palin's look before *she* did.
* Finally, Palin would go back to Washington and prove that she is willing to cross the aisle. John McCain already wants to pretend that George W. Bush doesn't exist. His running mate would just, you know, be helping him out. Besides, Bush's eyes already have the glazed look of a stuffed animal.

Moose that call the forty-ninth state home can breathe sighs of relief, but beware, homo sapiens. Some of you may be marked men and women!

#61 When Sarah Palin worked as a TV sports reporter for an NBC affiliate in Anchorage as a young woman, she modeled herself after the inimitable Howard Cosell.

Forget tea parties, playing with dolls, and learning to put on makeup. At an early age, Sarah Palin just wanted to be one of the boys: shooting guns, playing high school basketball, and now breaking the political glass ceiling. Her dream in high school was to sit in a broadcast booth with Howard Cosell.

At twenty-four years old, that dream came true, sort of.

After studying journalism in college, the avid sportswoman landed a job at KTUU-TV, Anchorage's NBC station, as a television sports anchor. Sarah Palin (known then as Sarah Heath) regularly offered all the highlights of local and national sports. Her sassy and spunky attitude was apparent even back then. In a report about the NHL, she said, "Minnesota's got to be notorious for something, I guess. They're the worst team in the NHL . . . they've got the worst record, anyway."

SARAH STAT

If you think she has big hair now, you should have seen her back in 1988! With some seriously high '80s bangs, too much eyeliner, large gold hoops, and a very distinct accent, our girl could have played an extra in Fargo.

HOBBIES & SPECIAL INTEREST (GROUPS)

While covering MLB news, she stated that legendary Dodgers manager Tommy Lasorda needed to learn how to relax! Now, now, play nice.

TOP TEN WAYS SARAH PALIN IS LIKE HER HERO, HOWARD COSELL

1. They both have/had bad hair.
2. They both know/knew how to throw a punch.
3. They both have/had voices like chalk on a chalkboard.
4. They both are/were, as the *New York Times* once said of Howard Cosell, "lighting rod[s] for criticism."
5. They both are/were unafraid of a good fight.
6. They both are/were survivors.
7. They are/were both fierce competitors.
8. They both fight/fought for what they believed, whether people liked it or not.
9. They both love/loved sports.
10. They both loved Howard Cosell.

POLITICS IS NO LAUGHING MATTER

"Matt Damon says Sarah Palin would be a disaster in the White House. I think I'll wait until I hear what Ben Affleck has to say."

DAVE LETTERMAN

Sarah Palin hates cats.

This according to members of Sarah's "Elite 6" (see #77 for more on them). On the other hand, animal aficionado John McCain has twenty-two pets in all, including a black-and-white cat named Oreo. In addition to the pussy, there's Sam the English springer spaniel, Coco the mutt, turtles Cuff and Link, a ferret, three parakeets, and thirteen saltwater fish. Perhaps he plucked the plucky Palin from Alaskan obscurity because of her Barracuda nickname, and thought she'd make a nice addition to his saltwater fish collection?

But is it McCain who loves animals, or his better half? One thing is for sure: This menagerie gives wife Cindy something to do all day long. Cindy referenced her devotion to their animals in *San Diego* magazine when asked what her husband would say was her most annoying habit.

"I guess I bring home stray anything," Cindy says. "Dogs . . . I love animals, so I'll wind up bringing strays home. I think that probably bothers him more than he says."

Perhaps McCain picked Palin to help him put an end to Cindy's penchant for "bringing strays home." Caribou Barbie could rid McCain of those pesky critters in no time.

So take cover, Oreo, Sam, Coco, Cuff, Link, et al. Palin's a good shot, you know, so don't take any chances. Stay in hiding until at least November 4. Polar bears, moose, and wolves should also go to higher ground.

Kinda gives a whole new meaning to the term "vetting."

#63 Allegedly, Sarah Palin sold singer Jewel, a fellow Alaskan, a used guitar.

While the transaction appears to have taken place on eBay, we have reason to believe that an outside agency might have been brought in to broker the deal.

Shortly after the guitar changed hands, we suspect Jewel attended Wasilla Assembly of God church and witnessed the erstwhile beauty queen speaking in tongues, which inspired the artist to revisit her roots and write a song in honor of Palin, which goes a little something like this:

SARAH STAT

Singer Jewel, well-known for living in her van and creating poetic lyrics to pop songs hails from Utah but spent her formative years living in Homer, AK (population: 5,364; known as a "quaint little drinking village with a fishing problem"). Jewel's grandfather, Yule Kilcher, was a state senator involved in drafting Alaska's constitution for its admission into a state from a territory in 1959.

Homer and Wasilla Are Magical Places
The scene is bleak, cold, snowy, harsh,
pregnant, homeless and addicted
Please promise me
We get by on snowmobiles, yodeling and church
For a 1,000 years

(continued)

Chorus:
Homer and Wasilla are magical places
with homesteaders in need of Wal-Marts
More than a million tears
A Barracuda, a book burner, a babe in glasses
Sometimes

Abstinence and hunting Palin Doctrine in Alaska
Remember forever more
I look forward to the Men in Trees, *Baked Alaska, the*
Iditarod, and yodeling some more
so special, boy its your....

Chorus (Reprise):
Homer and Wasilla are magical places
with homesteaders in need of Wal-Marts
I love it when we walk in the park
A Barracuda, a book burner, a babe in glasses
Remember forever more

POLITICS IS NO LAUGHING MATTER

"Joe Biden put his foot in his mouth the other day. Out campaigning, he told a crowd that Hillary is as qualified or more qualified that he is. Plus she still has her original hair."

JAY LENO

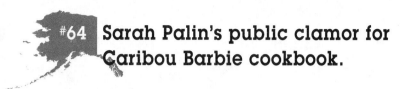

#64 Sarah Palin's public clamor for Caribou Barbie cookbook.

We're always hearing about how Sarah Palin hunts moose before breakfast for breakfast. But other than the recipes scattered throughout this very book, there's no public access to the treasured secret Heath/Palin family recipes.

If only she were to release a collection of her favorite game-based recipes—imagine how'd she'd further endear herself to the hearts and minds (and stomachs) of that critical hockey mom demographic.

These recipes would become part of every upstanding American mother's meals for her family. That is, as Palin defines family—one man, one woman, and one, or preferably more children, none of whom should have names previously used by human beings.

Palin's skills as uber Mom (tracking, skinning, chairing committees) are now well-known to the American public, yet her culinary abilities haven't received the same media attention.

Imagine how she might frame it: "Frankly, and everything I say is spoken frankly, I don't like to brag about my cooking, but so many of my friends have requested my recipes over the years that I feel it my duty to the nation to make them public," said Palin in a recent interview with *Shoot and Stab Quarterly*.

Palin could partner in this effort with the Alaskan chapter of the Ladies for a More American America (LMAA).

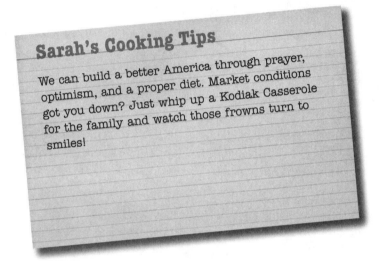

Sarah's Cooking Tips

We can build a better America through prayer, optimism, and a proper diet. Market conditions got you down? Just whip up a Kodiak Casserole for the family and watch those frowns turn to smiles!

RECIPES IN THE UPCOMING PUBLISHING
MINI-EVENT INCLUDE:
★ Moose Stew (see page 221 for a preview)
★ Moose Balls in Gravy
★ Caribou au Poivre
★ Muskeye and Wolverine with Field Greens
★ Kodiak Casserole
★ Pipeline Pie

#65 In 2005, Sarah Palin completed Humpy's Anchorage Marathon in 3:59:36.

Forget running the road to the White House, this frigid veep candidate made a mad dash across the frozen tundra in a marathon with runners that should be more concerned about hypothermia than dehydration. She clocked a fast enough time on the chilly course to rank fourteenth among women, fourth in her age group, and first in potential leaders of the free world.

SARAH PALIN: MARATHON WOMAN
One has to wonder how her skills on the course can translate into a potential political edge. Here's a quick look at how her fast feet might help McCain's agenda:

★ Well, it is a *run* for the White House.
★ Odds are at least one of them will survive to run again in 2012.
★ Runners are typically very healthy—if McCain needs someone to give up left lung and limb for him, she's his organ donor.
★ Forget never having traveled to Africa, Palin has much more in common with all of Nigeria than Biden could ever dream.
★ Don't you feel a *little* safer knowing your VP could outrun Oprah (4:29:20), Katie Holmes (5:29:58), and P. Diddy (4:14:54)?

THE POLITICAL RACE

Palin isn't the only elected official to put her Nikes where her mouth is and beat the pavement for 26.2 miles. While under four hours is a pretty impressive time, she's got some stiff, athletic competition if there's ever a *Battle of the Political Stars*. Here's how she stacks up against some other presidential- and VP-hopeful hoofers:

1. John Edwards, 3:30:18
   (Marine Corps Marathon, 1983)
2. George W. Bush, 3:44:52
   (Houston Marathon, 1993)
3. Sarah Palin, 3:59:36
   (Humpy's Anchorage Marathon, 2005)
4. Mike Huckabee, 4:39:04
   (Little Rock Marathon, 2005)
5. Al Gore, 4:58:25
   (Marine Corps Marathon, 1997)

It looks like Al Gore should stick to saving polar bears and leave running marathons to Caribou Barbie.

Part 10

THE ROAD TO NOWHERE—
OOPS, THE WHITE HOUSE

Sarah Palin's Cinderella-esque rise from obscurity to America's Right-Wing Sweetheart has her supporters cheering—and her detractors crying foul play.

MATT DAMON DISSES THE HOCKEY MOM

In an interview with the Associated Press, actor and political activist Matt Damon called the possibility of a Palin presidency " . . . a really scary thing." Citing McCain's age and history of health issues, Damon said there is a "one in three chance" that he will not survive his first term in office.

We wouldn't count on that, Matt. Actuary tables aside, McCain's mother is ninety-six years old and still going strong. In truth, she looks better than he does.

Damon then likened the scenario to a Disney film. "It's like a really bad Disney movie. The hockey mom . . . and she's president and facing down [Russian president] Vladimir Putin," Damon said. "It's absurd. It's totally absurd and I don't understand why more people aren't talking about it."

Wrong again, Matt. From what we can tell, everybody's talking about it. Indeed, it's virtually all anybody's talking about.

But back to showbiz. If Sarah Palin's life were to be a Disney movie, what kind of movie would it be? Now *there's* a campaign question really worth pondering. We pitched the following Palin projects to developers at Disney. We have yet to hear back.

COMING SOON TO A THEATER NEAR YOU . . .

★ *Mrs. Hockey Mom Goes to Washington:* Just like the Jimmy Stewart classic *Mr. Smith Goes to Washington.* Only with lots more lipstick.

★ *Barracuda:* Think *Jaws,* only scarier.

★ *Beauty and the Beast:* A live-action version of the animated film, in which the Beast doesn't turn into a handsome prince. He just fades away.

★ *The Little Moose Girl:* Recalls the tearjerker *The Little Match Girl,* only with a happier ending. Except for the moose.

★ *The Lady and the Tramp Daughter: Lady and the Tramp,* only with people—and this time the baby comes at the beginning of the movie.

★ *Bambi for Dinner:* Just like the original children's film, only Bambi dies for the sake of supper.

★ *The Great Moose Detective:* Think *The Great Mouse Detective* meets *The Deerhunter.*

★ *Finding Neo-Conservatives:* Just like *Finding Nemo,* only with right-wing fish.

★ *An Inconvenient Darwinian Truth:* Al Gore lectures the hockey mom on the Big Bang.

★ *Hunting for Columbine:* Thanks to our heroine Sarah, Michael Moore finds Jesus and takes up skeetshooting.

★ *Around the World in 80 Hours:* A documentary tracing Sarah Palin's trip abroad.

#67 When John McCain chose Sarah Palin for his running mate, everyone was surprised—including Palin.

He could have chosen anyone. Working with politicians from both sides of the aisle in Congress since 1986, John McCain had a variety of men and women to choose from for his Republican vice presidential nominee. He also had plenty of time to make the decision because his nomination was sealed up well before the formal nomination in September. The two most prominent candidates were Senator Joe Lieberman, McCain's good friend, and former Pennsylvania governor Tom Ridge.

But instead, McCain chose virtual unknown right-winger Sarah Palin, the governor of one of the most sparsely populated states in the Union.

WHAT A DIFFERENCE FOUR YEARS CAN MAKE

Lieberman and Ridge fit in with McCain, Model 2000—the one who "denounced the Christian right's Pat Robertson and the Rev. Jerry Falwell as 'agents of intolerance' who exercised an 'evil influence' over the Republican Party," as *The New York Times* reported. Lieberman and Ridge also were pro-choice.

Fast-forward four years. The McCain Model 2008 was designed to pander to the Christian right. To make up for his previous remarks about the Christian right, McCain even went as far as addressing the commencement at Falwell's Liberty University in 2006.

Although she was apparently McCain's third choice (after Lieberman and Ridge), Sarah Palin had everything that McCain Model 2008 could ever want. She is pro-Second Amendment, pro-life, pro-Christian—a neo-conservative's dream woman. She is, if you will, the Meg Ryan to McCain's very old Tom Hanks.

SARAH SAYS:

When asked if she hesitated when McCain asked her to be his running mate: "I answered him yes because I have the confidence in that readiness and knowing that you can't blink, you have to be wired in a way of being so committed to the mission, the mission that we're on, reform of this country and victory in the war, you can't blink. So I didn't blink then, even when asked to run as his running mate."

—SARAH PALIN

McCain and Palin present a new odd couple for the American people:

★ McCain did not support drilling for oil in the protected Alaskan National Wilderness Reserve; Palin does.
★ McCain serves as a ranking member of the Senate Committee on Armed Services and is a former POW; Palin has never served in the military.
★ McCain has been in Congress for more than twenty-five years; Palin has been a governor for twenty months. McCain was a teenage misfit back in the Dark Ages; Palin was a former beauty contestant from the big-hair 1980s.

TOP TEN ODD COUPLES IN POLITICS
1. John McCain and Sarah Palin
2. George W. Bush and Dick Cheney
3. Ted Kennedy and Mary Jo Kopechne
4. John Warner and Elizabeth Taylor
5. John F. Kennedy and Marilyn Monroe
6. Arnold Schwarzenegger and Maria Shriver
7. Ted Turner and Jane Fonda
8. Bill Clinton and Monica Lewinsky
9. FDR and Eleanor Roosevelt
10. Ike Eisenhower and Richard Nixon

Before her nomination, Sarah Palin played coy over her VP prospects.

Palin proclaimed that *she wasn't even sure what the vice president of the United States did* (besides controlling the strings of the puppet president). That was then. This is now. And naturally now that's she's gotten the veep nod from St. John of Arizona (with apologies to George F. Will), she's singing a very different (Heart) tune.

Nevertheless, the turnaround does beg the question: What *does* the vice president do, and if it's not very much, how will someone with Sarah Barracuda's high level of energy and need to accomplish things every day fill her time?

Of course her (running) mate won't be of any help. When the late Tim Russert of *Meet the Press* asked the Arizona senator back in March of 2000 whether he coveted the veep spot after the losing the Republican nomination to Dubya, Mr. Straight-Talk himself summed up his understanding of what a vice-president's duties entailed: "The vice president has two duties. One is to inquire daily as to the health of the president, and the other is to attend the funerals of Third World dictators. And neither of those do I find an enjoyable exercise."

Since it's a cinch that the hockey mom from Wasilla has a ton more energy than either Senator McCain or the dangerous old curmudgeon currently occupying the veep spot, we've decided to give some Guv-luv and help her out with a few suggestions.

READY, AIM, *FIRE*.

Target: Large, furry animals.

Weekly moose shoots out on the Capitol Mall!

READY, AIM, *FIRE*.

Target: Large political animals.

Put Palin in charge of firing the ideologically impure from government positions (just like Alberto Gonzales let the equally qualified and equally ideologically pure and equally high-energy Monica Goodling do over at the Justice Department).

Since there are so many moderates, liberals, and other godless types loafing around not putting terrorists in jail, not listening to unwarranted wire-tapped conversations, and not erecting the Ten Commandments on courthouse lawns, that ought to fill quite a bit of her time. After all, she fired all but one of the management-level staff in the city government

SARAH SAYS:

"As for that VP talk all the time, I'll tell you, I still can't answer that question until somebody answers for me what is it exactly that the VP does every day?"

—ALASKA GOVERNOR SARAH PALIN
IN A CNN INTERVIEW, JULY 2008

of Wasilla within six months of taking office as mayor, and cut an equally wide pink-slipped swath through the state of Alaska's ranks once she became governor (except for that ex-brother-in-law she couldn't *quite* get canned), so no one can complain that she lacks "experience" in this area!

READY, STEADY, *RUN.*
Target: Five-minute miles.
Let Coach Palin oversee the physical fitness of the Washington, D.C.–area Secret Service detachment by leading them on daily five-mile runs.

READY, STEADY, *SELL.*
Target: D.C. pork.
Palin can cut government "waste" by listing such "outdated" buildings as the Commerce Department, the Education Department, and the National Archives on Zillo and eBay! Yes, we know the Declaration of Independence and the Constitution are housed over there, but hey, who's really even paying any attention to those "guidelines" anymore anyway? That sort of thing is *sooo* 1999!

#69 Sarah Palin and Joe Biden agree that Barack Obama should have chosen Hillary Clinton as his running mate.

Rivals Sarah Palin and Joe Biden have one thing in common: They both think that Barack Obama regrets not having picked Hillary for his running mate.

> *"Make no mistake," Biden said at a rally in New Hampshire, "Hillary Clinton is as qualified or more qualified than I am to be vice president of the United States of America."*

SARAH SAYS:

"I think he's regretting not picking her now, I do," she said of Mr. Obama. She then praised Mrs. Clinton: *"What determination and grit, and even grace, through some tough shots that were fired her way, she handled those well."*

—SARAH PALIN

Palin's motives for saying Obama should have chosen Hillary were probably less noble. In an obvious effort to woo Clinton supporters, Palin has also said that Obama made a mistake by not choosing her as his running mate.

This shared opinion of the opposing VP candidates, however unlikely, is predictably the last we'll see during this election. Why? Because the two opponents could not be more different. And their public service records bear that out.

PALIN VERSUS BIDEN

Biden: Considered an expert in foreign relations
Palin: Can see Russia from her deck

Biden: Served in the Senate for more than thirty-five years
Palin: Once served dinner to more than thirty-five guests

Biden: Authored the Second Chance Act, designed to provide the tools convicts need to re-enter society successfully
Palin: Once gave second chance to "bad boy" boyfriend in high school

Biden: Has passed aggressive antidrug legislation
Palin: Once reportedly passed out after smoking a "fatty"

Biden: Wrote the groundbreaking Violence Against Women Act
Palin: Owns too many guns to worry about someone messing with her

#70 In her much-anticipated interview with Charlie Gibson on *ABC News*, Palin obviously stumbled when he asked her about the "Bush Doctrine," leading many pundits to speculate that she didn't understand the question.

THE *WHO* DOCTRINE?

When Charles Gibson of ABC asked Sarah Palin how she felt about the "Bush Doctrine," our hockey mom proved a little out of her element.

"In what respect, Charlie?"

Translation: What is the Bush Doctrine? S—t, I hope he doesn't notice that I have no f—king clue what he is talking about! Maybe if I get all "folksy" and call him by his first name, he'll overlook that I am a complete moron.

Stunned that a vice presidential nominee and potential president wasn't familiar with the fundamental foreign policy philosophy of the current president, whose doctrine of "preemptive strikes" against nations that pose a threat led to a conflict in which her own son will participate, Gibson just asked her what she interpreted it to be.

Again, she waffled. "His world view."

Translation: Am I getting warm, Charlie? Give me a hint, pretty please.

Gibson gave in and told her what it was. Once our girl understood the question, she avoided answering it.

"Charlie, if there is legitimate and enough intelligence that tells us that a strike is imminent against American people, we have every right to defend our country," she began.

Translation: Now that I understand the question, Charlie, there's no way I'm going to answer it.

Palin proceeded to drone on with talking points so obviously evasive that the journalist complained that she had buried him in a "blizzard of words." Finally, Gibson asked, "Is that a yes? That you think we have the right to go across the border with or without the approval of the Pakistani government, to go after terrorists who are in the Waziristan area?"

But Caribou Barbie did not let "Charlie" push her around. "I believe that America has to exercise all options in order to stop the terrorists who are hell-bent on destroying America and our allies. We have got to have all options out there on the table."

Translation: NANANANANA! You can't make me say it! You can't make me say it! You can't make me say it!

TOP FIVE MOST LIKELY PLACES THE
REPUBLICANS WILL INVADE IN 2009

1. Iran
2. Pakistan
3. Russia
4. North Korea
5. The White House

Not very funny, is it?

#71 The announcement of Sarah Palin as Republican nominee for vice president has initiated the creation and sale of merchandise. It might actually jumpstart the economy.

Trendhunter magazine reports that Palin's choice of eyewear has set off a buying frenzy among women who would "kill a caribou" for a pair of the same "I'm-sexy-*and*-serious" specs worn by Governor Palin. Cleverly based on the Kawasaki 704 series of frames and colored a fabulous Republican 34 gray, the price tag on this custom eyewear starts at $375 for the frames and, with lenses, tops out at about $700. A vision, indeed.

GET OUT YOUR CREDIT CARD

But that's only the tip of the Alaskan iceberg. Café Press, one of the largest web-based T-shirt and clothing retailers in the United States, has reportedly created 311,000 products bearing Palin's name, image, quotes, or related comments. Included in the selection are several varieties of thong.

Seriously.

Shoppers have a choice of the double entendre delight "Read My Lipstick, McCain Palin 2008"; the environmentally unfriendly but oh-so-pleasurable "Drill Baby Drill"; and the devout, yet tempting "Holy of Holies."

Word has it that Barack Obama, Joe Biden, and John McCain are all rather jealous, given the dearth of politically embellished jock straps.

FOR KIDS OF ALL AGES!
But let's not forget the kiddies. Herobuilders.com now has three Sarah Palin action figures available (see page 176)! You can stay home and play with the standard "Road to the White House" doll, decked out in a classy black pants suit. Or you can fight crime with the Sarah Palin "Superhero" action figure, disguised in a *Matrix*-style black coat and sexy white hot pants, with a nifty gun holstered to her thigh like Lara Croft.

THE POPE WOULD BE PROUD
There's even a toy for the more . . . dare we say it . . . liberal among us? Give your Ken doll a heart attack by introducing him to the Sarah Palin "Schoolgirl" figure, complete with Catholic school uniform, including plaid skirt, red bra and tight white shirt with tails tied at the waist. Grrr. No matter that Palin's not Catholic. She's not qualified to be vice president and no one seems to care about that either.

More than 500 Sarah Palin action figures were sold the first day they were made available.

Caribou Barbie would be cute, but these dolls are fierce. (Fierce like a pitbull. A pitbull with lipstick.) Now you can have your very own Sarah Palin action figure, in three varieties:

★ Executive ($27.95)—Featuring a slim, suited Palin at six months pregnant
★ Schoolgirl ($29.95) —Featuring Palin as she promotes teen abstinence
★ Pistol-packing superhero ($29.95)—Featuring Palin as Charlie's Angel with an updo

There's more to Palin than a short skirt and a garter-belt holster. We eagerly await:

★ The Miss Wasilla action figure—Complete with fake smile, ruffled dress, and bad '80s perm
★ The Couture Camo action figure—Complete with rifle, NRA membership card, and moose carcass (Charlton Heston action figure sold separately)
★ The Tina Fey as Sarah Palin action figures—Complete with *SNL* stage set and extra glasses

But, the point is: Here's your chance to have a piece of Plastic Palin, so you should order your very own before they're sold out! At least two different online outlets are hawking these twelve-inch tall dolls, with twenty-one points of articulation. "Be the talk of your neighborhood with this one-of-a-kind Sarah Palin action figure," exclaims one vendor (*www.sarahpalinactionfigure.com*).

You know good little Republican boys and girls will be the envy of their leftie friends when Santa brings them the desirable Palin dolls and the Dems stick their kids with these second-rate politicians, available from Herobuilders.com:

★ Eliot Spitzer ("Client No. 9")
★ Barack Obama ("Beach Blanket Obama")
★ John McCain (Plush, plastic, and Pez dispenser)
★ John Edwards ("Rogue")
★ Hillary Clinton ("Hillbilly")
★ Rudy Guiliani ("America's Mayor")
★ Dick Cheney ("You Don't Know Dick")
★ Howard Dean ("Mean Dean")

Evidently Joe Biden isn't important enough for a doll. Rumor has it, it would be too tough to fabricate hair plugs that small.

#73 Sarah Palin is being called "Cheney with lipstick" by her detractors.

At least, we *think* they're her detractors.

OR IS SHE THE NEXT QUAYLE?

Palin has been compared to other VP picks in history such as Dan Quayle and Geraldine Ferraro due to her low profile on the political stage. But she is also being compared to Dick Cheney, and is often labeled by Democrats as "Dick Cheney with lipstick," particularly because of her similarly conservative stance on social issues. Personally, we think the "pitbull" imagine is far more attractive.

Senator John Kerry feels the same. "With the choice of Governor Palin, it's now the third term of Dick Cheney, because what he's done is he's chosen somebody who actually doesn't believe that climate change is manmade," Kerry said. But Dick is pleased with the new VP pick. "Each administration is different," he said. "And there's no reason why Sarah Palin can't be a successful vice president in a McCain administration."

SARAH STAT

Get your Dick Cheney with lipstick mug or T-shirt at: *http://mugs.cafepress .com/item/palin-equals- cheney-with-lipstick-large- mug/302867331*

PALIN VERSUS CHENEY: A COMPARISON

Palin	Cheney
Hunts caribou	Hunts human beings
Opposes abortion	Looks like he survived one
Believes homosexuality is not genetic	Gave birth to gay daughter
Believes homosexuality is a sin	Feels same but has gay daughter
Believes in abstinence before marriage	Couldn't find anyone willing to have sex with him
Believes global warming is not manmade	Lives underground in the bunker
Wanted to take polar bears off endangered species list to promote drilling in Alaska*	Feels ambivalent. Loves oil but is half polar bear himself

* Note: According to AP reporter Dan Joling at www.dailykos
.com, Palin planned to sue the federal government "to challenge the
recent listing of polar bears as a threatened species," fearing that
the listing would "cripple oil and gas development in prime polar
bear habitat off the state's northern and northwestern coasts."

#74 Sarah Palin beats Dan Quayle for least-qualified vice presidential pick.

Suddenly, James Danforth Quayle is looking a lot better. That's not to say we don't still feel queasy when we recall him:

★ Comparing himself to John F. Kennedy . . .
★ Or insisting to a New Jersey elementary school student that he had misspelled potato ("potatoe") . . .
★ Or blaming the L.A. riots and society's demise on *Murphy Brown*, a fictitious TV newswoman who had a baby out of wedlock.

He was famous for his bumbling blunders and doubletalk a la Dubya ("I love California, I practically grew up in Phoenix") and during his time in office with Bush Sr., he worked diligently to promote his position as our nation's intellectual lightweight.

But how does our girl Sarah compare?

A mere two years ago, this beauty queen with a degree cobbled from five no-name universities, a self-described pitbull with lipstick was merely a small-town mayor of Alaska's crystal meth capital. (So much for Just Say No.) Evidently this is the kind of resume that lands you in the governor's office up there in half-baked Alaska. Sarah spent less than two years living in that governor's mansion when John McCain (with some urgent urging from Gold Rush Limbaugh, see #85) plucked her out of obscurity to shake up his anemic run for the White House.

Unfortunately, with Quayle's four years in Congress and eight years in the Senate, he just can't compare to our girl Sarah. According to Fox News Channel's Steve Doocy, "She does know about international relations because she is right up there in Alaska, right next door to Russia." To which Jon Stewart quipped, "When you think about it, Alaska is also near the North Pole, so she must also be friends with Santa."

SARAH SAYS:

"I've been so focused on state government, I haven't really focused much on the war in Iraq."

—SARAH PALIN, IN AN INTERVIEW WITH *ALASKA BUSINESS MONTHLY* SHORTLY AFTER SHE TOOK OFFICE IN 2007

"It's great to see another part of the country."

—SARAH PALIN, WHILE CAMPAIGNING IN PENNSYLVANIA

#75 As VP on the Republican ticket, Sarah Palin is expected to help convince those 18 million disaffected Hillary Clinton supporters to switch to the McCain camp.

According to Palin, "... Hillary left 18 million cracks in the highest, hardest glass ceiling in America, but it turns out the women of America aren't finished yet and we can shatter that glass ceiling once and for all." If Sarah does indeed help McCain attract some embittered Hillary supporters, it could spell victory for the Grand Old Party come November 4. But how much do Hillary voters and Palin supporters *really* have in common? Let's take a look at how they truly match up.

Hillary Supporters:	Palin Supporters:
Believe in global warming	Like their summers hot and wet
Protect our national forests	Just leave enough trees to cover hunting blinds
Provide universal health care	Not in favor of giving the universe health care—America first!
Teach evolution in schools	Are still evolving—slowly

Hillary Supporters:	Palin Supporters:
Support a woman's right to choose	Real women have a baby a year until they drop dead of exhaustion
Support comprehensive sex ed	Let kids find out about the consequences of unprotected sex the, uh, hard way
Believe in equal pay for men and women	Believe the same—but need God's opinion on the matter before they pay up
Believe that what is good for the geese is good for the gander	Believe that shooting geese is good for dinner

Pineapple and Teriyaki Goose Appetizers

Yields 24

Similar to rumaki, this is an excellent way to prepare goose breast for party fare.

1 boneless, skinless goose breast half

¼ cup teriyaki sauce

¼ cup hoisin sauce

1 tablespoon toasted sesame oil

12 bacon strips, halved

24 small pineapple chunks

(continued)

1. Preheat oven to 500°F.
2. Cut breast meat into 1-inch cubes. Place in a bowl. Stir in teriyaki sauce, hoisin sauce, and sesame oil. Marinate, refrigerated, for 1 hour.
3. Lay bacon strip halves flat. Place a piece of goose and a pineapple chunk on one end of bacon and roll up. Secure with a toothpick.
4. Bake in the hot oven for about 15 minutes, until bacon is crisp and goose is done.

Sarah's Cooking Tips

Pair these yummy goose-laden appetizers with bottle of warm saki and invite all the Hillary supporters you know over for a little Happy Hockey Mom Hour. They'll be swinging our way in no time!

Sarah Palin is not what Hillary voters are looking for, says Shirley MacLaine.

In this life or the next.

Academy Award–winning actress and bestselling author Shirley MacLaine says that it's "ridiculous" to consider Sexy Sarah a substitute for Hillary just because "she wears a skirt."

MacLaine's remarks come as no surprise, given that her world view is so different from Palin. She's New Age all the way, Palin's Christian hellfire and damnation all the way.

REINCARNATION OR HELL?

MacLaine does not believe in death, but rather in the "recycling of souls."

"That's why we have to question war," she says. "Who is being killed here? You just incur the energy of karma. And that's why we have to get into these different cultures and understand what they're talking about.

KARMA IN THIS LIFETIME

Evangelical Christian beliefs such as Palin's do not incorporate the idea of karma and reincarnation. Indeed, given Palin's apparent penchant for bloodsport both in the wild and in the political arena, we can only imagine what lives she's led in the past, and what karma Palin is building up for her next lifetime.

TOP TEN PAST LIVES FOR PALIN

1. Dick Cheney's mother
2. Attila the Hun
3. Phyllis Schlafly's mother
4. Paul Bunyan
5. John M. Browning
6. Diana, Goddess of the Hunt
7. Jimmy Swaggart
8. Eva Peron
9. Mata Hari
10. Pitbull

TOP TEN THINGS PALIN MIGHT COME BACK AS

1. Moose
2. New Yorker
3. Paleontologist
4. Unwed mother
5. Polar bear
6. Librarian
7. Gay man
8. Jewish gay man
9. Married Jewish gay man
10. Democrat

"The ancient cultures went into these questions," says MacLaine. "Our culture is so new we don't go into, especially new Christianity. . . . It's a subject that a lot of Western Christians don't like to discuss, because that robs them of this passionate idea of evil."

#77 Sarah Palin's best girlfriends, known as the Elite 6, are divided on whether to vote for her—or not.

Even Palin's buddies aren't so sure about her as a candidate for vice president. Her group of friends, who refer to themselves as the "Elite 6," met each other at aerobics classes.

"And we just kinda bonded and did our little workouts together, and after workouts, sometimes we'd go and have chocolate and coffee or soda," said Juanita Fuller, one of the members of the Elite 6 and a close friend of Palin.

WITH FRIENDS LIKE THESE . . .

Although they are Palin's pals, that doesn't guarantee her their vote. In an interview with *Good Morning America*, at least three of the four of the Elite 6 interviewed would not reveal who they would vote for.

"I support Sarah as a friend, and I can't necessarily say who I'm going to vote for," Elite member Patti Ricker said. "I haven't made up my mind yet. And, you know, I don't know what's going to happen. But, you know, I am pro-choice and I don't agree with everything Sarah says either. But, again, I haven't . . . committed to voting for anybody. I haven't decided yet."

Another member, Sandy Hoest, said that she disagreed with some of Palin's decisions as governor, including trying to sue the government for putting the polar bears on the endangered species list, where she says they belong. But she still hasn't made up her mind. "I have never voted for a Republican for president. And this may be the first time I vote Republican for president. I'm real excited to see the debates and make up my mind. But . . . I'm not committed."

Only Fuller said Palin was her choice. "I believe that she will help the nation go forward. She would help us in ways that would make us a better country."

DISCRETION IS THE BETTER PART OF FRIENDSHIP

Amy Hansen summed up how most of the women felt. "My vote is very personal. It is between me and the voting booth. So I'm keeping my mouth shut on that one."

YOU MIGHT BE AN ELITIST IN ALASKA IF . . .

★ You have all your teeth.
★ You have a car, house, *or* job.
★ You can name at least four of the "Lower 48."
★ You have been to college. Not necessarily enrolled, but just "been."
★ You have the luxury of eating "cooked" moose meat.
★ You do oxycontin and cocaine.
★ You hunt with a gun, not a spear.
★ You ride a snowmobile instead of a moose.
★ You read *Call of the Wild* (instead of just seeing the movie).
★ You can read.

Barack Obama takes heat for "pig in lipstick" remark on the campaign trail.

Obama says he was talking about change—or the lack thereof on McCain and Palin's platform. "You know, you can put lipstick on a pig," Obama said, "but it's still a pig."

Innocent or not, in the wake of Palin's "pitbull in lipstick" joke at the Republican National Convention, the Democratic crowd roared its approval—and Obama was stuck like a pig in s—t. He tried to set the record straight, adding, "You can wrap an old fish in a piece of paper called 'change.' It's still gonna stink after eight years."

Stink is right. The stink that followed leads us to wonder what this election is really about: Life after Bush . . . or Lipstick?

THE GOP GIRLS ATTACK

Jane Swift, former Republican governor of Massachusetts, was quick to denounce Obama, and insist on an apology on behalf of the McCain campaign.

"It's disgraceful. Senator Obama owes Governor Palin an apology," Swift said.

"This is just the latest in a series of comments that females like me will find offensive. . . . There's only one woman in the race. It's hard to think this was directed at anybody other than Governor Palin."

A PIG BY ANY OTHER NAME

Yet the "pig in lipstick" expression is one often favored by politicians—including McCain himself, who used it when denouncing Hillary Clinton's health care plan last October.

In fact, politicians often use such "folksy" animal expressions to endear their public—and show that they're one of them. Which may show that they're as sexist, racist, homophobic, intolerant, and ignorant as you and me.

TOP FIVE ANIMAL EXPRESSIONS POLITICIANS SHOULD NEVER USE

1. HORSE—Common expression: Rode hard and put up wet. *As in:* Pinch-faced Cindy McCain looks like she's been rode hard and put up wet.
2. HORSE—Common expression: F—k you and the horse you road in on. *As in:* What Hillary might be thinking whenever Palin "compliments" her.
3. DOG—Common expression: That dog don't hunt. *As in:* Living in Alaska doesn't make you a national security expert just because it's "close to Russia."
4. COW—Common expression: Why buy the cow when you can get the milk for free? *As in:* What Levi Johnston must have been thinking before he knocked up Bristol Palin.
5. DUCK—Common expression: If it looks like a duck, and quacks like a duck, it's a duck. *As in:* Why people are also calling Sarah Palin "Dick Cheney in lipstick."

Wild Boar Butt with
Barley and Sauerkraut

Serves
6–8

Big game loin roast or chuck steak can be substituted for the butt.
Serve with German-style grain mustard and crusty rye bread.

1 (3- to 4-pound) wild boar butt	2 bay leaves
½ quarts sauerkraut, rinsed and drained	½ teaspoon ground pepper
2 onions, thinly sliced	2 bottles beer, wheat or pale ale
½ cup pearl barley, rinsed and drained	¼ cup German-style mustard
	2–3 cups water

1. Preheat oven to 350°F.
2. Place boar in a Dutch oven. Top with sauerkraut, onions, and barley. Tuck in bay leaves and grind pepper over top. Pour beer over boar, then stir in mustard. Add water to the top of the sauerkraut (about 2 to 3 cups).
3. Cover and bake for 3 hours. Remove boar, slice, and serve on a platter surrounded with the sauerkraut and barley.

Sarahs's Cooking Tips

There are wild boars, and then there are wild pigs
or feral hogs. Runaway domestics are what these
animals are. They are also known as razorbacks
because they developed razor tusks and hair
on their backs after reproducing in the wild for
several generations. They are much smaller than
big boars. The best-tasting animals usually weigh
40–80 pounds. Avoid anything larger—unless you
shoot it yourself. Whatever the big wild boars may
lack in taste they make up for in taxidermy!

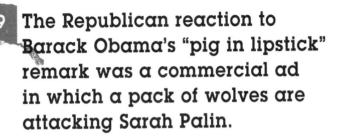

#79 The Republican reaction to Barack Obama's "pig in lipstick" remark was a commercial ad in which a pack of wolves are attacking Sarah Palin.

We don't know which moron on the Republican campaign trail is creating and running the ads, but at least he's a moron with a sense of irony—if not outright humor.

IT'S THE WOLVES' TURN

Wolves have fewer enemies more fierce than Sarah Palin. As a moose and caribou hunter, she doesn't want to compete with the wolves for dinner—even though wolves mostly scavenge their meat, rather than knock it off with a bullet between the eyes. Palin has supported some of the harshest decimation of the wolf population in memory—including a $150 bounty per severed wolf paw (later overturned by a state judge)—see page 8 for more on this benevolent policy of hers.

Knowing this, when you see a pack of wolves circling Caribou Barbie, you can't help but root for the wolves.

THE DEMOCRATS CLOSE IN

The Democrats were quick to respond to the Wolves Attacking Palin ad with a web video of their own. It offsets the McCain ad with another similar Wolves Attacking ad used by President Bush against Democrat John F. Kerry in 2004. In a split screen, voters see both ads, the one with wolves going after Palin and the ones using wolves to represent the security threats facing the United States at the time (the implication being that Kerry wasn't up to the task).

At the end, voters see McCain and Bush side by side "approving" their message, along with this sentiment:

"Same old tactics. Same old policies. Four more years?"

Again, wolves are painted as the aggressors. In a blood-sport as ruthless as this 2008 election campaign is proving to be, it seems the wolves—and the voters—don't stand a chance.

#80 Palin refused to conduct more interviews unless treated with "respect and deference."

Poor little Caribou Barbie. She's had a rough time with the press. They did terrible things, like question her on whether she has the experience to be a heartbeat away from the presidency, and even went so far as to ask questions about her family, including her pregnant teenage daughter and her (reportedly) drug-addicted son. Looks like when the pit-bull schtick doesn't work, it's time to go back to the hockey mom—even if you're not that good at it.

TAKE YOUR GUNS AND GO HOME

Rick Davis, campaign manager for McCain, said Palin won't do more interviews until she is treated with "respect and deference." Isn't that the kind of "whining" she accused Hillary of just a few months ago?

Call us cynics, but we suspect that this is just an excuse to keep Palin in a sound bubble so McCain and his aides will have time to prepare her for the debates, which she won't be able to weasel out of. They have a tough job ahead of them. She's got to learn the difference between a private company and a state-run company, why it might not be a good idea at this time to go to war with Russia, and where exactly she misplaced her brain.

SHAME ON THE BIG, BAD PRESS

So when can we expect out little sweet hockey mom to talk to the big bad press wolves?

"When we think it's time and when she feels comfortable doing it. Sarah Palin will have the opportunity to speak to the American people," said Davis. She will do interviews, but she'll do them on "the terms and conditions" the campaign decides.

Well, whenever she's ready. We wouldn't want to hurt her feelings, now, would we?

SARAH SAYS:

"When I hear a statement like that coming from a woman candidate [Hillary Clinton] with any kind of perceived whine about that excess criticism or, you know, maybe a sharper microscope put on her, I think, man, that doesn't do us any good. Women in politics, women in general wanting to progress this country. I don't think it's, it bodes well for her—a statement like that."

—SARAH PALIN, ASSESSING HILLARY CLINTON'S TAKE ON SEXISM DURING THE PRIMARIES

TOP TEN QUESTIONS MCCAIN CAMP IS
AFRAID PRESS WILL ASK PALIN

1. What is black and white and read all over?
2. What color was George Washington's white horse?
3. Why would WWIII be a bad thing?
4. Where is Iraq?
5. How many doughnuts are in a baker's dozen?
6. What is your son's favorite drug?
7. What is your favorite meal after a tough day of "snowmachining"?
8. Why is Barack Obama the Devil incarnate?
9. What is a dinosaur and when did they live?
10. 2 + 2 = ?

TOP TEN QUESTIONS PALIN CAN ANSWER

1. What is the difference between a pitbull and a hockey mom?
2. Why do polar bears suck?
3. Do abstinence programs really work? (feel free to draw on personal experience if necessary)
4. Why does God hate non-Christians?
5. What is better to say to win votes: raise taxes or lower taxes?
6. Why is McCain the most courageous person in history?
7. Are you proud that you grew up in a small town?
8. What kind of shoes are you wearing?
9. What is your favorite color?
10. What the f—k is so great about Alaska?

#81 In the wake of Sarah Palin's refusal to grant any more interviews until treated with "respect and deference," Papa Pitbull Karl Rove criticizes both parties for attack ads that go "too far" during this hotly contested 2008 presidential campaign.

Getting nailed by Karl Rove for unfair tactics is like getting nailed for anti-Semitism by Hitler. So maybe Palin and her fellow running mates should show a little respect and deference toward one another before they start demanding it of others.

When it comes to attack ads, Karl Rove is the original pitbull, sans lipstick. Rove made his reputation for being the nastiest man in politics as the ruthless power behind the George W. Bush campaigns. No surprise that it was an ad the Democrats ran calling McCain out for not using e-mail that Rove singled out.

"His war injuries keep him from being able to use a keyboard. He can't type. You know, it's like saying he can't do jumpingjacks," Rove said. McCain is a Vietnam War veteran and former POW.

But Rove didn't stop there, where he might have been expected to stop. He went on to call the McCain camp on the carpet as well.

"McCain has gone in some of his ads—similarly gone one step too far and sort of attributing to Obama things that are, you know, beyond the 100-percent-truth test," Rove told *Fox News.*

A KINDER, GENTLER POLITICS?

Rove had these words of advice for Democrats and Republicans alike. "They don't need to attack each other in this way," Rove said. "They have legitimate points to make about each other."

TOP TEN SIGNS YOU'VE GONE TOO FAR
1. You call your opponent a 'ho.
2. You call your opponent's spouse a 'ho.
3. You call your opponent's mother a 'ho.
4. You make fun of his or her wooden leg.
5. You boil the family bunny.
6. You post fake sex video of your opponent having sex with spouse on the Internet.
7. You post fake sex video of your opponent having sex with someone else's spouse on the Internet.
8. You post fake sex video of your opponent having sex with dog on the Internet.
9. You hire a call girl to seduce your opponent's teenaged son.
10. You hire a call boy to seduce your opponent's teenaged son.

Sarah Palin's bid for the vice presidency has unsurprisingly generated no end of debate and criticism. But what does surprise is the generally excellent quality of said criticism.

Consider the pointed, elegant statement made by philosopher, actress, humanitarian, and potential flotation device Pamela Anderson:

"I can't stand her. She can suck it."

Yes, the wisdom here is clear. Much like Rousseau, Franklin, or Cromwell, Anderson has swept away the detritus of ramshackle debate and honed in on the one true thing that matters. She has, in a word (or two), "nailed it." And in high heels, no less.

If only statecraft of such high caliber came so easily to those in Washington. It leads to the most obvious of questions: Why didn't Barack Obama choose Pamela Anderson to be his running mate rather than dull, slow-witted Joe Biden? Think of the possibilities. The Obama/Anderson ticket could go head-to-head with McCain/Palin more effectively and would certainly get more press coverage.

Pamela Anderson is an ex-*Playboy* playmate. She's buddies with Hugh Hefner. She effectively wielded big guns on her fabulous TV show *V.I.P.* (Come to think of it, big guns were everywhere on that show.) There's no doubt that she'd be able to carry the unthinking, beer-guzzling, "I-like-the-hot-chick" vote currently owned by Palin.

And while Palin likes to actually kill the things she shoots at, Anderson is a member of PETA. So she doesn't like to kill things, see? At least not animals.

But here's the clincher: Palin wants to eventually be president. And that's terrifying. Anderson just wants to keep looking hot. And maybe destroy a mink farm or a chinchilla ranch every now and then.

How can you not vote for that?

In related news, a recent letter signed by more than 150 scientists urges Governor Palin to exercise sound conservation and management of Alaska's wildlife.

But as far as Sarah's concerned, all those eggheads can just suck it.

SARAH STAT

Defenders magazine reports that "In the latest battle against wildlife in Alaska, Governor Sarah Palin proposed a new bill that would make it even easier to kill wolves and bears." The bill "fails to acknowledge the role carnivores play in keeping ecosystems healthy."

Defenders' Alaska associate Tom Banks notes that, "The state needs to pass wildlife management laws that are based in science, are economically feasible, address all user groups, and have widespread public support."

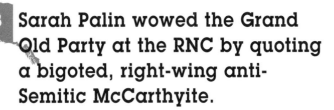

#83 Sarah Palin wowed the Grand Old Party at the RNC by quoting a bigoted, right-wing anti-Semitic McCarthyite.

"I guess a small-town mayor is sort of like a 'community organizer,' except that you have actual responsibilities."

"Know the difference between a hockey mom and a pitbull? Lipstick."

—Sarah Palin in her speech accepting
the Republican party's vice presidential
nomination, September, 2008

And with the above speech, a star was born.

Governor Sarah Palin of Alaska accepted St. John of Arizona's offer to join him on the Republican ticket, and in her speech accepting that nomination, she energized the Republican party's conservative base.

This should surprise no one who has learned anything about Sarah Palin. Depending on your politics, her speech showed confidence or arrogance, moxie or smugness, pride in simple American virtues or the sort of willful anti-intellectualism that would make the current tenant of 1600 Pennsylvania Avenue beam as brightly as a south Texas prairie brushfire.

No matter which side of the coin you fall on, you've got to give her this: She might not know much, but what she knows, she knows down to her manicured toenails, and second, she doesn't lack for guts.

And she gives a hell of a (scripted) speech. The question is, who scripted it?

WHO'S WALLACE PEGLER AND WHY QUOTE HIM ON TV?

In her speech, Palin singled out a previous vice president who had risen to the office of president upon the death of his predecessor, Democrat Harry S. Truman. In lauding "Give 'Em Hell, Harry"'s accomplishments, she quoted an unnamed author who supposedly spoke admiringly of Truman, and was quoted as saying: "we grow good people in our small towns, with honesty, sincerity, and dignity."

Since America's favorite hockey mom was trying to appeal to her audiences rather than repel them, she was pretty smart to give the name of the author of the quote in question. The person who wrote it was Wallace Pegler, bigoted right-wing anti-Semite and longtime supporter of "Witch-Hunter Joe" McCarthy during the fifties.

Oh, and he loathed Truman.

84

Sarah Palin and her hockey mom sex appeal injected the energy McCain needed to rile up the troops at the RNC.

Feet were stomping, hands clapping, throats were hoarse from yelling. Delegates waved American flags by the barrelful. Parents held children aloft to look over the sea of bobbing hands and upturned faces.

And we don't mean for the "star" of the show, Old Man McCain. We mean the world's sexiest second banana since Anna Nicole Smith.

Republicans wore buttons that said, "The hottest governor from the coolest state." And the voices coalesced into a chant: "Sarah! Sarah! Sarah!"

THE RNC HEATS UP

Before the announcement of Sarah Palin as John McCain's running mate, the Republican National Convention seemed headed for disaster—or at least for boredom. Hurricane Gustav cast a pall over the gathering; no one could figure out a way to politely tell President Bush that he was as welcome at the convention as a condom salesman in the Vatican, and delegates were less than inspired by the party's candidate, John McCain. They wanted red meat. They wanted a cultural warrior. They wanted to say, to hell with reason, and good manners, and issues, and all those boring things. We want a candidate who appeals to our guts.

ENTER THE RED MEAT MAMA

They got one with Sarah Palin. True, they also got a candidate who doesn't know what the Bush Doctrine is, didn't have a passport before a year and a half ago, is under an ethics investigation, is out of touch with mainstream American thought on issues like abortion rights, and has foreign policy expertise that consists entirely of being able to see Russia on a clear day across the Bering Straits. But they didn't care about any of that stuff.

"Omigod, she's so hot!" enthused one male convention goer. Others looked with envy at Palin's husband Todd (a former member of the Alaskan Independence Party, which wants to split off the state from the rest of the union—see #23).

IT'S WHAT YOU SAY; IT'S HOW YOU SAY IT

Palin's speech to the convention was notable for its tone as much as its content. John McCain might have promised to run a civil campaign that focused on issues and not personalities, but it was clear that Palin and her speech writers had tossed that idea out the window.

In fact even before the speech, Rick Davis, McCain's campaign manager, made clear what the campaign was about: "This election is not about issues," said Davis. "This election is about a composite view of what people take away from these candidates."

85

Rush Limbaugh turns to mush over Sarah Palin.

For months, Rush has been promoting Sarah Palin on his popular, conservative syndicated radio program, and back in February went so far as to design a McCain-Palin logo and post it on his homepage. Now that's conservative commitment. Something Rush thinks McCain could use a lesson in, but that's neither here nor there . . .

After showing lukewarm support of McCain in the months leading up to the RNC, Rush is now wholeheartedly endorsing the ticket because of his girl Sarah. As noted by several online commentators, a casual observer listening to these interviews with Rush might think Ronald Reagan had risen from the dead and was running for vice president in 2008. "I did not want that to end last night. . . . I didn't want the night to end. What a night! Folks, we have a future beyond November here. Regardless what happens. . . . Properly executed, beautifully articulated. . . . This lady has turned it all around. . . . From now on, on this program John McCain will be known as John McBrilliant."

RUSH TO THE WHITE HOUSE? JUST SAY YES!

But is this just one elaborate, choreographed act to take over the White House? Rush is pretty sure neither John McCain nor the First Dude will fare well in the Beltway. This just extends his GOP high, in which he figures he'll get the girl, call the shots, procure cheap prescription meds to feed his Jones. His record on this matter is clear:

★ "Too many whites are getting away with drug use. . . . Too many whites are getting away with drug sales. . . . The answer is to go out and find the ones who are getting away with it, convict them, and send them up the river, too." —Limbaugh in 1995
★ "I am addicted to prescription pain medication." —Limbaugh in 2003
★ "Did you know that the White House drug test is multiple choice?" —Limbaugh, date unknown

In fact, we think Rush has already enlisted the soon-to-be First Son to help him get his hands on some cheap oxy, sent priority from the backwaters of Alaska.

#86 Sarah Palin courts the minority vote on her way to the White House.

Sarah Palin is a new voice for the minorities in this country. Note: We didn't say a *positive* voice for minorities, but a voice nonetheless. Much like her international relations with Russia (closest U.S. state to Russia! Eat that, California!), Palin has a similar experience with minorities. Out of the 663,000 citizens of Alaska, 4.7 percent are African Americans, so we can assume that she *had* seen a black person prior to encountering Barack Obama.

DON'T LET THE NUMBERS CONFUSE THE ISSUE

Democratic liberal elites from the northeast with their education and facts would make you believe that 75 percent of Alaskans are white and she is out of touch with the issues of the average minority citizen. However, that remaining 25 percent is enough for George Bush's approval rate, so why wouldn't it be good enough to believe in Sarah Palin? Actually, Bush's approval rating hovers around 30 percent, but who believes in numbers anyway? Democrats should know numbers betray them—more people voted for Al Gore than Bush in the 2000 presidential contest and Gore still lost. Now the numbers are down for Palin with minorities, and, all of a sudden, the Democrats want to rely on "numbers"? Shouldn't they instead have empathy for Palin?

Palin may support building a fence across Mexico to keep out Mexicans, but isn't she just protecting Mexicans who already are here from those illegal, homosexual, anti–Second Amendment immigrants who will take their jobs, homosexuals, and guns. Oh yeah, the liberals would make you believe she also wants the illegal immigrants already living here out of the country too, but those are just words.

And words are no more significant than numbers. Just ask the Republicans.

COUNT ON PALIN

So maybe John McCain and Sarah Palin are losing minorities by a small margin (the Republicans' mighty, gun-toting 22 percent to the Democrats' liberal elitist 70 percent) to Barack Obama and Joe Biden in the 2008 presidential election, but don't count them out yet. Palin's husband Todd is one-eighth Native American. The First Dude is living proof that Caribou Barbie knows how to win over minorities.

#87 McCain challenges Sarah Palin to woo swing states for the Grand Old Party.

This late in the campaign, Obama and McCain are targeting swing states to try to gather the most electoral votes to win the election. Having Sarah Palin aboard gives McCain an auspicious edge. It's been proven that voters are far more likely to vote for candidates who shares their likes, dislikes, and belief systems—or even anatomy.

YOU LIKE HER, YOU REALLY, REALLY LIKE HER!

Now, McCain is hoping to rein in the swing voters based on Palin's favorite activities and pastimes. Her Alaskan background and woodsy nature make Palin a natural at many of the activities enjoyed by citizens in states such as Minnesota, West Virginia, Ohio, and Florida.

THANK GOD FOR HUNTING SEASON

Moose hunting season opens in Minnesota in October—just in time for Palin to find common ground with swing voters. Those with a strong stomach have seen the pictures of Palin skinning her prey after the hunt and have heard of her aerial hunting policies where, according to the Humane Society's Wildlife Abuse Campaign (*www.hsus.org*), hunters "chase animals down to the point of exhaustion with a plane or helicopter and then shoot them."

Despite the fact that Alaskans have twice banned this practice, Palin's strong support will endear her to those Minnesotan voters who love to hunt. Setting up an aerial hunt and helping swing voters skin their prey is a sure-fire way to place Minnesota in the crosshairs of the McCain-Palin ticket!

SNOWMOBILER FOR VICE PRESIDENT!

Palin can employ a similar strategy in Colorado where snowmobiling is an immensely popular sport. According to the *LA Times*, Sarah's husband, Todd, a snowmobile racer, came in fourth place in the 2,000-mile Tesoro Iron Dog snowmobile race after breaking his arm 400 miles from the finish line.

At least as tough as her husband, Palin can certainly use her love of this outdoor activity to clinch the vote for McCain. Challenging Obama to a literal snowmobile race for votes could do wonders for Colorado. There's no way Palin would lose, and the money charged for tickets to the event could be donated to the National Snow and Ice Center, which alerts snowmobilers about dangerous avalanches. According to the University of Colorado in Boulder, Colorado has the highest rate of deaths by avalanche . . . with Alaska coming in second.

Now we're talking common ground.

Look out, Democrats, or you'll be lost in the avalanche of voters swinging to the McCain camp.

#88 **Many Americans, mostly Democrats, have voiced concerns over Sarah Palin and the difficulties she may face raising new baby, Trig Paxson Van Palin, while vice president.**

These critics have obviously not thought this situation through. Women in general, and mothers in particular, have long been known as excellent multitaskers. As the mother of five, Sarah Palin would bring superior multitasking skills to the job of vice president. Palin should not be thought of as an exception to this rule. Indeed, she may personify it!

WHO'S ALREADY UP AT 3 A.M.?

Moms with babies, that's who!

Hillary Clinton and Barack Obama spent months trying to prove that they were the candidate America would want to pick up the phone at 3 A.M. America chose Obama, but perhaps they should look in a different direction now. Think of it this way: Sarah Palin won't be groggy when dealing with a national crisis. She won't even have to get up to answer the phone. She'll already be up and wide awake feeding her newborn or rocking him to sleep. How hard can it be to make decisions that affect the

> SARAH STAT
>
> Everyone knows that men can only do one thing at a time. But women can do multiple things at a time, just like the country song "W*O*M*A*N" says.

lives of millions when dealing with a finicky baby? For Sarah
Palin, not hard at all!

FLYING TIME IS BONDING TIME

The president and vice president spend a lot of time on Air
Force One. Many children, infants especially, don't fare well
when flying, but Trig's short life has already been defined by
air travel. He was born after his mother made the eight-hour
flight from Dallas, Texas, to Anchorage, Alaska.

According to the *Fairbanks Daily News*, Palin "noticed
amniotic fluid prior to giving a keynote luncheon address at
the Republican Governor's Energy Conference in Texas. After
wrapping up the speech, Palin and her husband . . . proceeded
with the trek home." This airline relationship will ensure that
long flights on Air Force One will be a great time for Palin to
bond with her newborn son and will make important home-
land security decisions easy to make while she bounces her
baby to sleep.

ALL IN THE FAMILY

Important family time is also being spent as Palin uses her
children to help her and McCain win the election. According to the *Lowell Sun*, Palin held Trig following a speech
where she promised to help children with disabilities once
in the White House. Palin is also using her daughter to get
her viewpoints across on abortion and her son, a soldier, to
show her support for the war in Iraq. Some may call using
her family in this way unethical, but really it's just a way for

the Palin clan to spend some quality time together while their mom is on the campaign trail. Good for Sarah!

VOTE FOR MOM!

Given a mom's talent for multitasking, it's a wonder that we don't have more moms in office. If Sarah Palin can do it, why not *all* moms? Why not *my* mom? Why not *your* mom? After all, we know how bad dads are at multitasking . . . and yet we let them run the government.

TOP FIVE WAYS DADS MULTITASK
1. Rock baby in recliner and drink beer.
2. Feed baby a bottle in recliner and drink beer.
3. Order pizza for the kids and drink beer.
4. Play video games with Junior and drink beer.
5. Watch *Dirty Jobs* with kids and drink beer.

Part 11

ON STYLE AND
SEX APPEAL

89

As the mother of five, Sarah Palin is living proof that _someone_ is having sex in Wasilla. (Presumably with First Dude Todd Palin.)

That said, this could be considered a surprise, as it's not exactly the sexiest spot in America. Or even in Alaska.

In fact, take a close look at Wasilla, and you may wonder how anyone has sex there at all.

LET'S DO THE (TANTRIC) MATH
A full one-third of Wasilla's residents commute the forty-three miles to Anchorage for work, an hour's drive on a good day. An hour in the car in the morning and an hour in the car in the afternoon would easily drain away any pesky sexual urges that might develop in the course of a day. And it's hard to think in any great detail about sex when you have to scan the horizon for errant moose on the road, or try to avoid spilling hot coffee on your lap while the guy in the SUV next to you wanders into your lane in an early-morning stupor. By the time you've reached home every day, you'd be more ready for a beer than a leer.

COLD, COLDER, COLDEST
In defense against Wasilla's frigid weather, the residents of Wasilla are swathed and bundled under layers of warm clothing that also work against the idea of a fast romp. The average

temperature in January ranges from a chilly 4 degrees to . . .
29 below. That's right, 29 below. Not only is it difficult to find
the sexiness in your fellow humans when they are swimming
in layers of wool flannel, goose down, and Gortex, but should
you actually work up the energy to make a pass at someone,
how long would it actually take to undress and get busy? All
those buttons. All those zippers. All that long underwear.

IF YOU REALLY WANT TO GET LAID IN WASILLA, LEAVE

One famous Wasillian left town completely in order to pursue
sex. Porn star April Flowers (you can meet her—*really* meet
her—on *www.visitapril.com*) is proud to claim Wasilla as her
hometown. She did have to go all the way over to Anchorage,
though, before she learned to take her clothes off in a topless
bar. Another hearty Wasilla commuter.

What's the Most Popular Aphrodisiac in Wasilla?
A trip to Hawaii.

#90 Sarah Palin has gone on the record to say that moose stew is her favorite meal.

As we've established, Sarah Palin is a woman who eats moose for breakfast. And looks great. Amazing, actually, when you consider she's forty-four, has had five children, and is in politics—all of which may conspire against a girl's looking her best—she looks downright amazing.

Which leads us to the inevitable conclusion that sexy mother of five's beauty secret is this: Moose.

Who knew?

But hey, we're never one to look a gift moose in the mouth. So we're jumping on the moose beauty bandwagon in a big way by revealing the first and (as far as we know) only Mighty Moose Diet. Forget those Skinny Bitches and their vegan diets. The real key to staying fit and trim is moose meat. And lots of it. Just remember when you're as svelte as Sarah Palin that you saw it here first.

THE MIGHTY MOOSE DIET

This diet is based on the health-enhancing qualities of big game. Moose for sure, but also antelope, elk, bear, deer, caribou, wild pig, wild boar, javelin, buffalo, mountain goat, and sheep. You may substitute as you shoot and see fit.

The best part: You never get hungry. Whenever your stomach starts to growl, just help yourself to unlimited quantities of Moose Stew. You'll be amazed at its appetite-controlling qualities! *Note:* For best results, you should hunt the meat yourself. The exercise will do you good.

Breakfast
Moose and Egg-White Omelet
Biscuits
Coffee

Snack
Moose Jerky

Lunch
Moose Stew
Alaskan Giant Cabbage Coleslaw

Snack
Moose Jerky

Dinner   *OR*
Small Critter Casserole   Slow Cooker Roast of Moose
                          Salad Greens

Sarah's Cooking Tips

For a change of pace, the Mighty Moose Diet incorporates just small and big game. Alaskan hunters enjoy an abundant variety of wildlife here and have learned to hunt and cook many dishes from the bounty of wild game.

SARAH SAYS:

When asked to name her favorite meal: "Moose stew . . . after a long day of snowmobiling."

—SARAH PALIN, IN THE *ANCHORAGE DAILY NEWS*

Small Critter
Casserole

Serves
8

Serve this easy dish with crusty bread or spoon it over egg noodles or cooked rice. Tailor the vegetables to suit your own taste. Fancy it up with fresh mushrooms. A tablespoon or two of chopped fresh tarragon or thyme would be a nice addition, too. If it needs some extra zip, add a squeeze of fresh lemon juice and a pinch of red pepper flakes.

2 pounds small game meat, cut into 2-inch chunks*

1 cup seasoned flour

¼ cup vegetable oil, more if needed

1 (16-ounce) bag frozen mixed vegetables

1½ cups artichoke hearts, chopped

8–10 green onions, chopped

2 cups chicken stock

1 12-ounce can cream of celery soup

Kosher salt and freshly ground pepper to taste

1. Dredge meat in seasoned flour and brown in a skillet with ¼ cup vegetable oil. Brown in two batches so the pan is not overcrowded. Add more oil if needed.
2. Add vegetables, artichoke hearts, green onions, chicken stock, and celery soup. Cook over medium-high heat, stirring occasionally, until it just comes to a boil, about 12 to 15 minutes. Lower heat to a simmer, cover, and cook until meat is tender. Season to taste with salt and pepper.
3. Serve from the pot or transfer to a pretty serving bowl to serve family-style at the dinner table.

* Small game includes rabbit, hare, squirrel, raccoon, woodchuck, beaver, opossum, and muskrat.

Sexy Sarah's
Moose Stew

Serves
6

If you don't have easy access to moose meat, you can substitute venison, bison, or beef.

3 tablespoons vegetable oil

2 pounds moose meat, diced

1 large onion, finely diced

1 jalapeño pepper, minced

1 rib celery, diced

2 cloves garlic, minced

10 cups water or beef broth

2 carrots, trimmed and sliced

2 parsnips, trimmed and sliced

1 16-ounce can diced tomatoes

2 cups cooked wild rice

Salt and pepper to taste

Mighty Moose

Like most game meats, moose can be relatively mild or gamey, depending on the age of the animal and where it has been grazing. Unlike deer and bison, which are farmed and packaged for supermarkets, moose is still primarily the bounty of hunters. Nonhunters can satisfy their curiosity through online vendors.

1. In a deep skillet or Dutch oven, heat oil over medium-high heat. Working in batches, brown moose cubes. Remove browned cubes to a plate. Add onion, jalapeño, celery, and garlic to the pot. Sauté for 3 minutes.
2. Add broth and reserved meat to the pot. Bring to a boil, then reduce heat to medium. Add carrots, parsnips, and tomatoes to the pot and cook, stirring occasionally, for 2 hours.
3. Stir in rice and add salt and pepper to taste. Remove from heat and let stand 5 minutes before serving.

Slow Cooker Roast of Moose

This tender treatment of venison is perfect for making venison French dip sandwiches. Pile pulled meat onto a hoagie-style bun that has been buttered and toasted. Serve a small bowl of the hot au jus on the side for dipping. If there is not enough au jus, add 1 can of beef consommé to the juice and heat.

1 (5- to 6-pound) moose or other venison roast

3–4 cloves garlic, sliced

Kosher salt and freshly ground black pepper to taste

3 onions, peeled and thickly sliced

3 bay leaves

3 whole cloves

3 whole peppercorns

1½ cups hot water

1 tablespoon Worcestershire sauce

1 tablespoon soy sauce

1. Preheat oven broiler to high. Make small slits over roast and insert slices of garlic. Season with salt and pepper to taste. Broil for about 10 to 15 minutes.
2. Place one-third of the onion slices in the bottom of a slow cooker. Cover with roast. Add remaining ingredients. Cover and cook on low for about 10 to 12 hours or until meat is fork tender.
3. Serve pieces of roast with au jus.

#91 Sarah Palin's hairdo, which recalls the beehive of the 1960s, has created a furor among women and hairdressers across the land.

Alternately decried as provincial and applauded as sexy in a librarian kind of way, it's a look that Sarah Palin uses as a campaign strategy.

BEEHIVES ATTRACT BEES—AND SO MUCH MORE

It's called a beehive because its smooth, conical shape is similar to the shape of a natural beehive or wasps' nest. The style is also referred to as the B-52 since it resembles the smooth, bulbous nose of the classic bomber.

First created by Margaret Vinci Heldt in the mid-1950s, the hairstyle was wildly popular throughout the late 50s and early 60s. It was a time when big, elaborate styles were in fashion. Women routinely sported coifs reaching several inches tall or even greater than a full foot in height, often using hairpieces to add even more volume to their locks.

A variation tried out was the partial beehive, which leaves the back of the hair loose, falling about the shoulders, or deliberately leaves tendrils of hair loose to frame the face, helping soften the severity of a beehive.

HAIRSPRAY!

Our vice presidential candidate is going to need busloads of hairspray because that darling little beehive she likes to perch on her crown requires a true commitment to the time needed for upkeep, hairspray used to lacquer it in place, and blinders to fashion that allows a governor to think it's a happening hairdo. Apparently, fashion trends flow slowly to Alaska, because the beehive that singer Dusty Springfield popularized in the late 1960s actually lost its sheen by the early 1970s.

MIND THE BUGS!

Those in Palin's inner circle might want to stand a bit farther away as the week lengthens because beehives work best when Sarah hasn't washed her hair for three days. Also, if you notice your sexy vice president scratching, it might be more than dandruff that's causing her to push those pencil nubs into the center of the mound. Although we think it's urban legend, way back in the 1960s when beehives were last popular, some reported roaches nesting in their heavily lacquered, untended beehives. Also, just so you know, beehive proponents usually wrap the hive in a silk scarf at night to preserve the nest.

PUSHBACK REQUIRED!

You might take heart in knowing that our hockey mom will know how to push back. You see, in order to create that sassy beehive, she has to backcomb her hair, and then delicately smooth a few hairs over the top to hide the mess she's just created. Here's the tricky part: Backcombing damages her hair shafts. But here's the good news for you: This girl isn't afraid to damage the shaft to achieve the desired, if outdated, effect. And she'll plaster that beehive with lacquer to hold it in place.

Those skills might come in handy as vice president should we need someone to value appearance over nurturance or protection of natural materials—even her own natural materials. This woman will not be averse to drilling in her backyard or ignoring any calls for bans of harmful environmental pollutants.* And don't be surprised if she shows up one day sporting a tiara, which is considered the perfect hair accessory for a beehive.

Proponents of the beehive include:

★ Audrey Hepburn in *Breakfast at Tiffany's*.
★ Yeoman Janice Rand from the original 1960s *Star Trek* TV series (she wore a complex, "futuristic" version of a beehive).
★ Florence Jean Castleberry, played by Polly Holliday, from Cowtown, Texas, in the '70s TV series *Alice*. Castleberry wore her red hair in a beehive trimmed by a waitress visor.
★ Several of Gary Larson's female characters in *The Far Side* series, who almost exclusively wear the beehive.
★ The retro-rock/new wave group The B-52s, who derived their moniker from the hairstyle.

* *According to ImmuneWeb.org, benzyl acetate (which is found in perfume, cologne, shampoo, fabric softener, stickup air freshener, dishwashing liquid and detergent, soap, hairspray, bleach, after shave, and deodorants) is a carcinogenic (linked to pancreatic cancer). Its vapors have been known to irritate eyes and respiratory passages, exciting cough. In mice, it has caused hyperanemia of the lungs. It can also be absorbed through the skin, causing systemic effects.*

* Marge Simpson, who sports an extreme, two-foot-high, blue beehive.
* Patsy (Joanna Lumley) from the cult British TV series *Absolutely Fabulous,* who wears her hair almost exclusively in a beehive. In the episode "Fish Farm," she is shown styling her beehive with a fork.
* R&B/jazz singer (and infamous drug addict) Amy Winehouse, who is known for her beehive hairdo and wigs.
* Wilma Flintstone and Betty Rubble, who in the "Fred's New Boss" episode get their hair done in gigantic, elaborate beehives at a salon, and then drive their car very slowly to protect their hairdos. Unfortunately, their 'dos are destroyed after a fast-moving dinosaur vehicle passes by and blows them down.

WILL THE REAL FASHION ICON PLEASE STAND UP?

Let's take a look at the two sides of Palin's fashion world.

Frumpy	*F—k Me*
Mukluks	Go Go Boots
Camouflage	Cashmere
Long underwear	Thongs
Flannel shirts	Tube tops
Waders	Minis
Pantsuits	Pencil skirts
Parkas	Trench Coat
Bun	Down and dirty

#92 Sarah Palin believes that when it comes to politics, frumpy is better than fashionable.

There are both bonuses and drawbacks to having an also-ran beauty queen as your vice president. For one, she becomes facile at trying harder while denying that she's trying at all.

"I wish they'd stick with the issues instead of discussing my black go-go boots," she has famously said. "A reporter once asked me about it during the campaign, and I assured him I was trying to be as frumpy as I could by wearing my hair on top of my head and these schoolmarm glasses . . . I guess I was naïve, but when I hear people talk about it I just want to escort them back to the Neanderthal cave while we get down to business."

METHINKS PALIN DOTH PROTEST TOO MUCH

But that's not the way *People* magazine sees it: "To this day, she [Palin] is a fashion addict, favoring flashy high heels and Kazuo Kawasaki designer glasses . . ."

Whether you see Sexy Sarah as a fashion plus or a fashion minus, there's no doubt that she's already kicking off fads of her own, intentionally or not.

Bonus

You can always claim that she can single-handedly stimulate the economy. Orders for the Kazuo Kawasaki rimless glasses she wore when accepting the nomination quadrupled, benefiting Italee Optics, the U.S. distributor (whew). And WigSalon.com, a U.S. distributor (again, whew), is briskly selling Palin-style wigs and hair pieces, ranging from the $115 Raquel Welch "Valentine" style (which clever hockey moms can instantly transform into Governor Palin's beehive by pinning back the upper layers) to a $45 "Bargain Sarah Palin" wig in ginger brown that women can pin to their crowns.

Drawback

While your sexy vice president may be turning some nimble heads, setting trends among the masses (mindless masses, perhaps), not all retailers and manufacturers are going to fall into line. Shortly after our Sarah jokingly called Patagonia and North Face her "favorite designers," Patagonia, a company that harbors a strong environmental philosophy (it makes many of its clothes and shoes out of recycled materials), issued a statement saying it has "absolutely no plans" to promote its association with Mrs. Palin.

POSSIBLE ENDORSEMENTS?

Patagonia aside, not every fashion company will put principle before profit when it comes to Palin. She might find more luck with these:

★ Fur products
★ Flak jackets
★ Camouflage suspenders

★ Hunting boots
★ Wellies

#93 Sarah Palin is setting a new fashion standard, albeit not necessarily a high one.

She's no Jackie Kennedy. Despite the irrational rush to dress like Caribou Barbie that seems to have infected the unfashionable masses, your vice presidential candidate is at the opposite end of the fashion spectrum from the ultimate American style icon, aka Jackie Kennedy Onassis. Consider these contrasts in style:

Jackie: Pearls and diamonds
Sarah: Rhinestone tiaras

Jackie: Carefully coiffed pageboy
Sarah: Hastily coiffed beehive

Jackie: Tasteful pillbox hats
Sarah: Plaid hunting caps

Jackie: Classic black Roger Vivier designer pumps
Sarah: Spicy red Naughty Monkey peep-toe pumps

Jackie: An equestrian
Sarah: A moose hunter

Jackie: Classy intellectual debutant
Sarah: Feisty hockey mom

Jackie: Hosted tours of the White House
Sarah: Leads you down the road to nowhere

Jackie: Collects fine art
Sarah: Collects bear rugs

And just in case you didn't notice, she's a little bit country and a little bit funky. Those eye-catching Naughty Monkey red peep-toe pumps she wore when McCain announced her as his running mate typically appeal to twenty-something hotties who love to wear them clubbing—so whoo-hoo, brother McCain!

Also, even though her style—or lack thereof—will likely bring lots of attention, you might want to note the subtext: Anyone who owns red shoes is likely to flaunt a strong, outspoken, dynamic personality. It may well hold true that not since Paris handed that apple to Aphrodite has a man's selection of a woman had such implications for the future of our civilization.

#94 With her striking Tina Fey eyeglasses, Sarah Palin joins a long line of bespectacled politicians.

From monocles to wire-rims, our highest-ranking government officials have often required glasses to see clearly (or not). But not since Teddy Roosevelt has the eyewear of a vice presidential candidate caused such a fashion furor.

YOU'VE GOT SARAH PALIN EYES

Undeniably, Sarah's sexy librarian look comes in part from the spectacular spectacles. One of the most memorable parts of Palin's Republican National Convention speech, based upon viewer response, was her choice of eyewear, which captivated women across America. Her frames, designed by the Japanese eyewear guru Kazuo Kawasaki, are selling out all over the country. Optometrist telephones across the country were ringing off the hook with women who wanted a pair of "Sarah Palin glasses." The titanium frames start at $375 and they're part of Kawasaki's 704 series.

SARAH STAT

According to Essilor of America:

73 percent of Americans say glasses have no impact on attractiveness

68 percent of Americans whose lovers wear glasses say the spectacles don't affect intimacy

40 percent of Americans believe people wearing glasses are smart

39 percent of Americans believe people wearing glasses are sophisticated

#95 Sarah Palin recently announced that her favorite designer is Patagonia.

Her reasons for choosing this particular designer are not immediately obvious, particularly in view of the fact her choices in footwear match those of Paris Hilton, who is not known as environmentally minded. That said, there is a certain logic to the choice.

PATAGONIA: GREAT SOURCE OF CLOTHES AND HUNTING TIPS

Patagonia accomplishes more than commerce on their website, with information on a number of environmental issues (*www.patagonia.com*). Their blog "The Cleanest Line" includes the post "Polar Bears Swimming Amongst Melting Arctic Ice," and this is where the connection to the Gov becomes more clear. Palin undoubtedly considers the site a source of information and tips on hunting local wildlife as well as a supplier of outfits for the well-dressed field stalker.

PATAGONIA SHOOTS BACK

Any business would love to receive an endorsement from a public figure enjoying the media attention received recently by Governor Palin. Correct? Well, perhaps not.

Patagonia is a clothing manufacturer where the environment is considered a Big Deal.

"Patagonia's environmental mission greatly differs from Sarah Palin's," Patagonia rep Jen Rapp told the *Wall Street Journal*. "Just wearing the clothing of an environmental company does not necessarily make someone an environmentalist."

FASHION HUNT

Well, Jen, who's talking about the environment besides you? We're talking fashion and sneaking up on unwary prey. Those Patagonia women's vests, offering warmth without bulk and available in natural colors (camouflage is so passé!) are perfect for early morning hunts with the gals, dishing the dirt with the Elite Six, or picking up the kids at school in the SUV. And with the right accessories, you can transition easily into evening activities—pumps for dancing at the Elks Lodge, or a pump-action for twilight hunting.

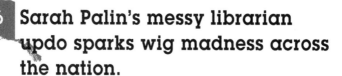

#96 Sarah Palin's messy librarian updo sparks wig madness across the nation.

And that's just the tip of the iceberg bun. WigSalon.com has watched in amazement as Sarah Palin–style wigs blow off their shelves. Shoe stores are experiencing runs on her style of shoes. (The shoes, incidentally, a red pair of open-toe pumps with three-and-a-half-inch heels, are part of the Naughty Monkey line of shoes produced by House of Brands. The company has sent out a picture of Palin wearing the shoes and the slogan "I vote for Naughty Monkey!")

Allure magazine, meanwhile, has suggested readers try lipstick colors that are "pitbull friendly" and "pig appropriate." (No, really!)

And in Alaska, Governor Palin is a well-known patron of the used-clothing store Out of the Closet, where she's friendly with the store management. This may account for what the *Los Angeles Times* referred to as her "no-nonsense" style, as opposed to the designer labels worn by Cindy McCain and Laura Bush. Note: Someone might want to explain to Sarah the common usage of "out of the closet."

Trend forecaster Tom Julian, who's reported on fashion at the Oscars for many years, says, "She should definitely not take her fashion cues from Cindy McCain, who is a totally couture, 7th Avenue fashion plate. Perhaps a line like

American designer Ralph Lauren would answer all Governor Palin's needs."

Or maybe she needs an outfit with wide cuffs, where she can jot down cribnotes for her interviews. Something big enough to hold an explanation of the Bush Doctrine.

TOP TEN REASONS TO WEAR A SARAH PALIN WIG

1. You're having a *really, really, really* bad hair day.
2. It's Halloween.
3. Your boyfriend thinks Tina Fey is really hot.
4. You're a trannie.
5. You need a disguise to meet your husband's partner for a tryst.
6. You're running for vice president.
7. You can't find a decent hairdresser in Alaska.
8. You want to play the Snowmobiler and the Sexy Librarian in bed.
9. You lost your Racquel Welch wig.
10. You're wearing your hockey mom hat today.

Part 12

SARAH PALIN:
2010

#97 John McCain's choice of vice presidential nominee might just end up presiding over the end of the world. Just ask the Mayans.

The average age at which our previous forty-three American presidents took office was 54.8 years. Should John McCain win in November, he will be the oldest person ever elected to a first-term presidency, at the age of seventy-two. (Ronald Reagan was sixty-nine.) According to the Mayo Clinic (*www.mayoclinic.com*) the average American male currently lives an average of 74.8 years.

SARAH PALIN: PROPHETESS OF DOOM?

What does all of this have to do with Sarah Palin? Well, let's face it, the presidency is not an easy job, and McCain doesn't have the best record as far as his health goes, including his well-known bouts with skin cancer. Should he die in office, Sarah Palin would become one of the youngest, most inexperienced presidents in U.S. history. And in 2012, she'd be up for reelection.

IT'S REALLY THE 2012 DATE THAT'S THE PROBLEM

You see, that's when everyone pretty much expects the world to end. And we're not just talking about the Mayans, although their wacky backward-counting calendar is the best-known neon sign pointing out the coming apocalypse. According to the bestselling book *The Bible Code* (available at your local bookstore for just $16), the earth is going to be hit by a big-ass comet. The exact words associated with the date of impact are "earth annihilated." The 2012 doomsayers who claim that 2012 will be a bad year to be in charge include:

★ That cheery old whack job Nostradamus ("The shaky peace on earth will be struck by fire from the skies . . . then will come a horrible slaughter of people and animals.")
★ Author and "scientist" Patrick Geryl ("I'm going to write some bestsellers about how you're all going to die, then I'm going to go hide in a cave.")
★ Self-appointed interpreter of God Vijay Kumar ("All of your scriptures are like Bazooka Bubblegum comic strips to me!")

TERMINATOR MOM
Let's hope, should Palin find herself in such an unenviable position of power, that her experience as a gun-totin' soccer mom gives us the edge we need to survive.

#98 Sarah Palin has said that she "didn't even blink" at the thought of being just a heartbeat away from the presidency.

Caribou Barbie may have complete confidence in her ability to serve as leader of the free world, but some of us are not yet convinced. Indeed, the prospect seems practically Orwellian.

We've joked about the possibility of a Palin actually becoming the president of the United States, but what if it really happened? What would our cute little pitbull do? What would Washington look like after she "cleans it up"? Certainly Washington, D.C., and the world would be a very different place should President Palin occupy the White House.

A MOOSE IN EVERY POT

Life with President Palin would mean an Alaskan Renaissance for the entire nation. There'd be a gun in every house and a moose in every pot. Families would hunt together, pray together, and shop for mukluks together. Abstinence programs would rule the day, and with abortions outlawed, the streets would be full of the sweet sounds of children playing, and their teenage moms crying. Everyone would drive SUVs with gunracks, and forego baseball in favor of hockey.

But President Palin wouldn't stop there. As America goes, so goes the world. If you play your cards right.

PALIN'S 12-STEP ACTION PLAN TO
WORLD DOMINATION

Step One	Ask God what to do.
Step Two	Continue with plan, since God isn't talking.
Step Three	Fire everyone in Congress, including Republicans, and replace them with robots that Palin can control at will to consolidate power. Supreme Court justices would unfortunately have to be killed.
Step Four	Fire all the librarians in the country, parade them around in shackles, and then burn them at the stake on the state-run Fox News television station—along with all those offensive books.
Step Five	Make carrying a handgun not only legal in fifty states, but mandatory in order to deter crime—and scare moose.
Step Six	Send elite special forces units to wipe out every polar bear in the world once and for all. Bastards!
Step Seven	Overturn *Roe v. Wade* to begrudge young women the same choice that her daughter had.
Step Eight	Officially change phrase from "American as apple pie" to "American as moose stew."
Step Nine	Make the "beehive" hairdo mandatory for women over forty.

Step Ten	Travel abroad—not to meet with leaders, but just because it might be fun for the kids. Charge the White House for the trips.
Step Eleven	Create giant cooling machine to be used from outer space just in case those atheist scientists are right about the warming trend.
Step Twelve	Ask someone who isn't an idiot what the hell she is supposed to do. Like Barack Obama.

PALIN'S WHITE HOUSE FOREIGN POLICY

Palin's foreign policy decisions would be consistent, and would illustrate American resolve. Here's what she would do—but not necessarily in this order:

* ★ Invade Iran
* ★ Invade Pakistan
* ★ Invade Russia
* ★ Invade South Korea
* ★ Invade Iraq—again.

#99 Palin and Bear Grylls make the perfect GOP ticket in 2012.

Everyone's already talking about Sarah Palin running for president in 2012. The assumption is that John McCain will step down should he still be president. That means Sarah Palin will need a new vice presidential candidate.

However, McCain's replacement has to have certain qualifications. This person has to have less experience than Palin, so she looks better by comparison. He or she has to have the rugged outdoorsmanship, the "I-can-bullshit-you-better-than-you-can-bullshit-me" attitude, and gross-out aspect that the blue-collar audience loves. The answer: Bear Grylls.

GET OUR BOY BEAR A GREEN CARD

First the obvious problem: He was born in the UK and isn't eligible to run for vice president. So, let me get this straight: American audiences allow the Welsh Christian Bales to play Batman, but they will have a problem with Grylls being the vice president? He just has to affect his fellow Brit Hugh Laurie's American accent in *House* and he's all set.

A MATCH MADE IN THE WILD!

Grylls is a born politician. While filming his show *Man vs. Wild*, Grylls has often stayed in motels, but told the audience that he was staying in the wild at night. This is going to come in very handy when dealing with the liberal media. Also, he has experience staging his exploits, but later claiming they are reality in the making. When America declares war against smaller countries, Grylls can stage it so the war takes a longer time than it actually does; this would provide the new administration with money that they could use for anything else, similar to Palin's experience with the "Bridge to Nowhere."

Just imagine the PR potential! Palin and Grylls hunting together. Palin and Grylls urinating on their clothes to protect them from the sun. Palin and Grylls grilling (if we're lucky) their catch or Palin and Grylls chowing down their catch raw (if we're not so lucky).

PALIN AND GRYLLS'S TOP TEN SURVIVAL TIPS

1. Use Palin's makeup mirror to signal planes for help.
2. Cut up that Patagonia credit card and use it to cut moose.
3. Filter nasty water through Caribou Barbie's bra.
4. Use lipstick to write SOS on rocks, car hoods, or pigs.
5. Crush one of Sarah's tampons and use the cotton inside as kindling.
6. Take the laces off the hockey mom's mukluks and use them to tie together branches in a lean-to.
7. Use her sock to filter water as well.
8. Use Sarah's wristwatch as a compass.
9. Magnetize one of her government report's paper clips and use as a compass.
10. Take Sarah's flashlight battery and cross with wire to ignite a fire.

#100 Hollywood producers are all scrambling to cast *The Sarah Palin Story*.

Almost the first thing that happens to anyone who becomes famous these days? She gets an agent. The second thing is? She sells film rights.

Somewhere in a Hollywood office right now, executives are frantically cobbling together a pitch for *The Sarah Palin Story*. La-la Land being what it is, one can only imagine their casting choices:

SARAH PALIN: Tina Fey
(fresh from her triumph on *Saturday Night Live*)
TODD PALIN: Tom Selleck
(for rugged, manly, Alaskan good looks—slightly used)
JOHN MCCAIN: Jon Voight
CINDY MCCAIN: Barbie®
BRISTOL PALIN: Britney Spears
LEVI JOHNSTON: Kevin Federline (Come on!
You knew these two were going to get together again!)
DEAD, SKINNED MOOSE: Courtney Love
GEORGE W. BUSH: Dana Carvey
Produced by the Grand Old Party
Directed by Steve Schmidt
Bigger than Bush! Wilder than Swiftboating!
Filmed entirely in RedStateVision

When zombies attack the Earth, Sarah Palin will save us.

As governor of Alaska, Sarah Palin has the potential to be the leader of the only zombie-free state. Imagine what she could do as vice president. That's right—if the events of *Resident Evil: Extinction* come true, then Palin truly would be the only hope for humanity.

TAKE THAT, YOU ZOMBIE BASTARDS!

Palin is really the ideal person to lead us. Gee, what kills zombies? Oh, that's right, a bullet to the head! She shoots moose, just think what she'd do to zombies!

With her environment making her blood as cold as her soul, Palin is pretty much zombieproof. As everybody knows, zombies hate cold blood. Think about it: The brain is really delicious with a warm, gravy-like blood coating, but when that blood is cold, the brain's flavor and substance suffers. Zombies would be repulsed by the thought of eating Alaskan brain.

FORGET HURRICANE KATRINA, WE'RE TALKING ZOMBIES HERE

Granted, the Bush Administration has mishandled national disasters, but this is Sarah "I kill my meat, watch it slowly die, and then eat it" Palin. If she saw her citizens being desecrated by zombies, Palin would blow those zombies away!

She would also educate the zombies. The fact that zombies don't reproduce would not stop Palin from teaching them about abstinence. Also, she would teach them that they should correct their brain-eating ways because when Jesus Christ comes back, they will face his wrath!

VOTE DEMOCRATIC AND YOU'LL DIE BY ZOMBIE!

Liberals could never deal with those infected by the virus. These wimps would not only fail to fight back, they'd seek to sanctify the marriage between zombies and American citizens. They'd pass equal pay for equal work for zombies. They'd even hand out green cards.

Remember: if you don't vote Palin, you support zombies, and that is just plain un-American.

Not to mention dead.

SOURCES

www.246.com

http://abcnews.go.com

www.adfg.state.ak.us

www.adn.com

www.boston.com

www.cdc.gov

www.dailykos.com

www.fieldandstream.com

www.foxnews.com

www.gawker.com

http://gov.state.ak.us

www.huffingtonpost.com

www.latimes.com

http://mccain.senate.gov

www.motherjones.com

www.nationalenquirer.com

http://news.bostonherald.com

www.newsweek.com

www.newyorktimes.com

www.nfwf.org

www.OKmagazine.com

www.people.com

www.politico.com

www.theodoreroosevelt.org

www.timesonline.co.uk

www.vanityfair.com

www.washingtonpost.com

www.wasillaag.org

www.wasillabible.org

www.wikipedia.com

www.youtube.com

THANKS AND APOLOGIES

We'd like to thank our contributors, without whom this book would not have been possible. We'd also like to thank everyone at Adams Media, most especially Laura Daly, Colleen Cunningham, Brendan O'Neill, Susan Beale, Frank Rivera, Beth Gissinger, Karen Cooper, Matt LeBlanc, Stephanie Bernardo, and last but never least, Sara Domville and David Nussbaum.

We'd also like to take this opportunity to apologize to: the people of the great state of Alaska, hockey moms, soccer moms, Republicans, Democrats, Pentecostals, the Elite Six, Sarah Palin, First Dude Todd Palin, Bristol Palin, Track Palin, Trig Palin, Piper Palin, Willow Palin, Levi Johnston, ~~George W. Bush~~, John McCain, Hillary Clinton, Tina Fey, Eve Ensler, Barack Obama, Joe Biden, Cindy McCain, Laura Bush, Michelle Obama, the people of Wasilla, Alaska, the Palin family, Sally and Chuck Heath, Sandra Bullock, ~~Wal-Mart~~, moose, polar bears, wolves, caribou, beaver, pitbulls, the Wilson sisters, ~~Dan Quayle~~, ~~Karl Rove~~, the people of the great state of Idaho, ~~Creationists~~, Theists, Naturalists, scientists, paleontologists, Ivana Trump, Donald Trump, unwed mothers, stoned teenagers, congregants of the Wasilla Bible Church and the Wasilla Assembly of God, gays, lesbians, our men and women serving in Iraq and Afghanistan, dinosaurs, Irl Stambough, ~~moonshiners~~, ~~the NRA~~, Pentecostals, Elvis Presley, Jerry Lee Lewis, ~~Jimmy Swaggart~~, Jim and Tammy Faye Bakker, ~~James Watt~~, ~~John Ashcroft~~, ~~Oral Roberts~~, T.D. Jakes, G. Gordon Liddy, Richard M. Nixon, Iditarod mushers, the people of Kuwait, the people of Iraq, Native Americans, African Americans, feminists, ~~FOX News~~, Charlie Gibson, ABC News, Jon Stewart, ~~British Petroleum~~, Dave Letterman, Jay Leno, Conan O'Brien, ~~Dick Cheney~~, Nancy Pelosi, the B-52s, Matt Damon, Ben Affleck, Jewel, John Kerry, ~~Pastor Ed Kalnins~~, Jesus Christ, Britain, Ireland, Spain, Germany, Ellen Page, Teddy Roosevelt, ~~John Edwards~~, Mike Huckabee, Disney, Ted Kennedy, Monica Lewinsky, Elizabeth Taylor, and Bill Clinton.

CONTRIBUTORS

Brian Thornton
Skye Alexander
Ben Malisow
T. S. Winn
Justin Cord Hayes
Wendy Simard
Brendan O'Neill
Hillary Thompson

Stephen D. Rogers
Phil Sexton
Peter Archer
Andrea Norville
Susan Reynolds
Matthew Glazer
Richard Wallace
Katie Corcoran Lytle

ABOUT THE AUTHORS

Writer and comedian GREGORY BERGMAN (Los Angeles, CA) is the author of *WTF?*, *BizzWords*, *-Isms*, and *The Little Book of Bathroom Philosophy*. He might just vote for Sarah Palin, because she's one hot MILF of a politician. But don't tell his Sisterhood of the Traveling Pantsuits mother.

PAULA MUNIER (Boston, MA) is a veteran writer and editor. Army brat and the mother of three, grandmother of one, she could shoot guns, run 5Ks, and ban books with the rest of the Caribou Barbies any time if she so chose. But she chooses not to.